The Liverpool Competition

A study of the development of Cricket on Merseyside

by

P.N. Walker

Cover Design: ERIC R. MONKS

Acknowledgements

I must thank the following people for their invaluable assistance, in allowing me to interview and quote them and in providing material: Tom Law and Arnie Martin (Bootle C.C.), Frank Hack (Chester Boughton Hall C.C.), Lionel Lister (Formby C.C.), Bill Adams (Hightown C.C.), Harry Owen (Huyton C.C.), Jack Bennett (Liverpool C.C.), Charlie Swift (Neston C.C.), Ken Lea (Ormskirk C.C.), Peter Burrell (Oxton C.C.), Eric Tatlock (St. Helens C.C.), Ken Porter and Frank Cartwright (Southport and Birkdale C.C.), Harold Wolfe (Wallasey C.C.), and Mrs. Stubbs (Archivist at Pilkingtons).

This book was originally researched as a dissertation in 1983 for the University of Liverpool's Diploma in Local History, and I am grateful for the invaluable assistance given me at that time by Paul Booth and Merfyn Jones.

First published 1988 by Countyvise Limited, 1 & 3 Grove Road, Rock Ferry, Birkenhead, Wirral, Merseyside L42 3XS.

Copyright © P.N. Walker, 1988.
Photoset and printed by Birkenhead Press Limited, 1 & 3 Grove Road, Rock Ferry, Birkenhead, Merseyside L42 3XS.

ISBN 0 907768 16 4

Content

Introduction

This book attempts to trace the development of cricket on Merseyside and to explain the rather unique quality of that loose federation of clubs known collectively as the Liverpool Competition. Many of these clubs have written a history, often produced on the occasion of their centenary. Some are very well researched and beautifully produced, whilst others are little more than accounts of famous matches of the past, together with a heavy lacing of local advertisements which were no doubt essential in defraying the printing costs. They are nearly all rather brief and, not surprisingly, subjective histories which highlight the best qualities of each club. I have not attempted to rewrite or replace these, but rather to supplement them and, by looking at the clubs as an outsider and placing the events in the social context of their times, to identify the influences which may have determined the way in which they developed.

There are a considerable number of cricket clubs within the area which I have taken to be Merseyside. This is not the strict administrative area, but also includes all the Wirral down to Chester and Ormskirk. Exactly how many is not important, but as an example, there are within the Southport boundary twelve clubs, one each in the Liverpool Competition and the Merseyside Competition and ten playing in the local Southport and District League.

It may then appear unfair to choose the senior clubs of the area, those of the Liverpool Competition, to study and to suggest that their development is characteristic of the sport on Merseyside. For example, one immediate distinction is that they were and, to some extent, still are clubs for the middle classes, whereas the smaller clubs, especially those from the local leagues, have catered more for the working man.

There are, however, several reasons for this choice which more than justify the class-biased picture which may emerge. First, they are the principal clubs because the standard of cricket they play nowadays is far and away the best, although this may not always have been the case for all of them. This is not to say that the junior clubs have not produced cricketers of a high standard, but rather these men have either chosen to remain big fishes in small pools or, more especially since the last war, moved to one of the Competition clubs. The opportunity for them to take this latter course has varied from club to club and from time to time.

The second and more obvious reason for the choice is that selection of some sort is essential for the study to be more than a cursory one. Clearly it would have been foolish to choose clubs, associations or leagues with which I was unfamiliar and with whom I had few contacts.

Thirdly, there is their longevity; all the Competition clubs with the exception of Hightown (1908) are products of the 19th century. Whilst they may not always have enjoyed their present elevated status, they have survived, some of them for more than 150 years. Many of them have dominated the game on Merseyside for well over a century and it is surely to these that we must look to determine any pattern. As Christopher Brooke has pointed out, "It is to the dominant forms of the game that one must look to find the source of the impetus".[1]

A wide range of sources was consulted. Much of the secondary material came from general local histories and club histories, although I have made extensive use of oral history, the views and memories of men who played in the Competition in earlier days. Among the wealth of primary evidence which I discovered or which the clubs provided for me, the most useful and informative were the minute books of the clubs' committees, but much could also be gleaned from old scorebooks, account books, scrapbooks, letters and newspapers.

Some of the clubs had so little information about their early history, that useful research, given limited time, proved impossible and I, eventually, studied only ten of the 16 in any detail. Of these I chose to examine and write about six of them, partly because of the wealth of source material and partly because each was, in its own way, particularly interesting.

I have tried to pursue a different theme in each chapter, both to highlight the ways in which each club was unique and also to demonstrate that many of them had common problems and lines of development. The first chapter shows how Liverpool C.C. became the principal club and, to a great extent, the model for many of the others. With Bootle and Ormskirk, I have attempted to show the similarities in their early struggles and to emphasise the differences caused by their respective urban and rural settings. Southport and Birkdale C.C. was chosen not so much for any unique quality, but as an example of how one club made its position secure. In contrast St. Helens Recs. C.C. was unique, and not only on Merseyside, as the first recreation club to be set up by an industrial employer. The chapter on Huyton C.C. , the last club chosen, shows how the fortunes of a club can rise and fall and examines to what extent this was beyond their control. The final chapter, on the professionals, gave me the opportunity to bring in several of the other Competition clubs, whilst looking at the often fascinating life styles and careers of these men and the attitudes of the clubs towards them.[2]

Note

1) C. Brooks, *English Cricket* (Weidenfeld and Nicholson, 1978), p.8.
2) Some of my material in Chapter 2 has been used in the club brochures of Bootle (1983) and Ormskirk (1985).

CHAPTER ONE
The Dominant Influence — Liverpool C.C.

If the Liverpool Competition can be said to have been the dominant force in the development of cricket on Merseyside, Liverpool C.C. surely dominated the other clubs within it. For this reason as well as the fact that it dates from 1807 and is therefore the oldest existing club in the area, any history of local cricket must start with Liverpool.

By the time Liverpool C.C. had settled at its present site in Aigburth in 1881, cricket had become a major part of English social life.

> "It was no accident that during the 19th century expressions like 'to play with a straight bat' and 'it's not cricket' became almost liturgical. The sentiments they echoed clearly reflected the upper class values, which by this time dominated the game."[1]

It is possible in the southern counties to trace how this had come about, how cricket had developed from a folk game played by ordinary people in rural 16th and 17th century England, how it had declined as a result of urbanisation, industrialisation and the fewer opportunities for leisure and how this decline had been stemmed by the adoption of the sport by gentlemen with their seemingly limitless amounts of leisure time. In the north-west, however, there is no evidence of such development. The folk or village variety of the game, if it ever existed here, must simply have disappeared. Its growth seems to have come about not as in the south of England by the patronage and participation of the landed gentry, but rather through groups of gentlemen of commerce who wished to play cricket recognising it as an activity befitting a gentleman. As Liverpool grew, so too did its commercial connections with the south and the capital. Most probably it was such contact that persuaded the 30 gentlemen to join together to form "The Original and Unrivalled Mosslake Fields Cricket Society" in 1807. There is a reference to a game of cricket having been played in Cazneau Street prior to 1800 but no details as to whether it was more than just an impromptu occasion.[2]

The rules of this 'Society' are worth setting down as they give some indication of the social position of the members and of their keenness.

> "First. That every member on admission to this Society, by signing these rules, shall pay to the Treasurer the sum of seven shillings to be considered a part of the General Fund.

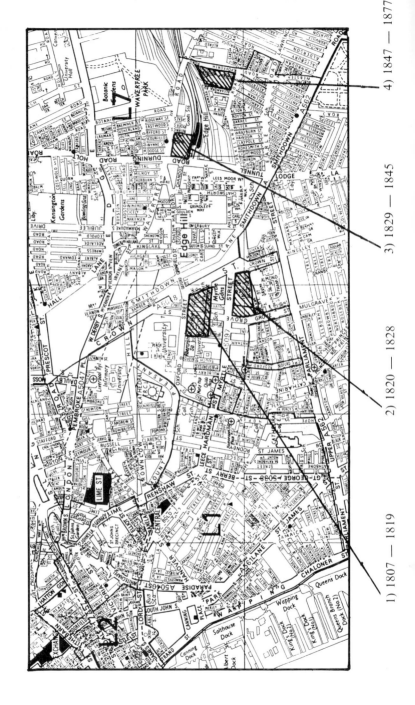

Locations of the early Liverpool Cricket Club Grounds.

4) 1847 — 1877

3) 1829 — 1845

2) 1820 — 1828

1) 1807 — 1819

Second. That every of the undersigned members assembled on the field appropriated to their use in Mosslake fields, on the mornings of Monday, Wednesday and Friday, in each week during the present season or so long as a majority for the time being may think proper to keep the said Society on foot.

Third. That 6 o'clock be and is hereby fixed the hour of attendance on every such mornings and every member who shall be absent from the field at a quarter past six o'clock shall be fined in the sum of sixpence. If halfpast six one shilling. If seven o'clock one shilling and sixpence and in the case of non-attendance (except as aftermentioned) the sum of two shillings.

Fourth. That all Fines shall be received by the Treasurer who shall appropriate the same to the use of the Society and be considered as part of the General Fund.

Fifth. That there be a President elected every month who shall have the privilege of choosing a Treasurer.

Sixth. That every dispute which may arise in this Society whether within the field or without shall be decided by a majority of members present in which the President has two votes.

Seventh. That no excuse be admitted for non-attendance in any respect unless occasioned by business or sickness in which case notice shall be given to the President or some member who shall next meeting report the same.

Eight. That all fines unpaid within three days after they shall be incurred shall be doubled, if six days trebled and if unpaid at the end of nine days the members so minus shall be dismissed by the Society.

Ninth. That any member shall be at liberty to resign but after his resignation he shall not be admitted again without first paying his entrance money of seven shillings."[3]

These rules were aimed obviously at ensuring the full participation and co-operation of each of the members and say little about what the Club's objectives were nor whom they would play against. This, of course, is one of the imponderables. As the first known cricket club in the area, one might imagine that it had been formed to play against some opposition. Although there are records of the existence of clubs in Yorkshire and Derbyshire before this time,[4] it seems unlikely that apart from on a very rare occasion, these could have been the opposition. Sheer distance, before the railways, would have precluded such ventures. Most probably they were content to play most, if not all, of their matches among themselves. Indeed 40 years later this was still largely the practice.

Clearly the 30 gentlemen were sufficiently affluent to afford a seven shilling subscription, yet the hour at which they chose to gather for practice suggests that the majority were not of the leisured classes. 6 o'clock in the morning also suggests that their season was a relatively short one, since the light would not be good enough except in the period May to August.

In the Gore's Directory of 1807 only five of these men can with any certainty be identified. These were David Rees, a merchant of Brownlow Hill, David Stewart, a surveyor of Warren Street, the brothers John and Joseph Cheesbrough both accountants of Basnett Street and George N. Hardey a provision merchant of Westmoreland Place. Probably the remainder were young men who were either not working or not sufficiently established in their occupations to warrant being included in the directory.[5]

This tends to be confirmed by looking at a later Directory, that of 1818. In this a further seven can reasonably be identified. Nathan Litherland book-keeper, Joseph Threlfall merchant, J.R.F. Rowlinson and Charles Rowlinson both attorneys, Robert Edmondson gentleman and John D. Stewart merchant.[6] The remainder are either unlisted or their names are so common, like Jones, Parry and Hughes, as to make identification impossible.

It is difficult to draw conclusions from this other than to suggest that they were for the most part, young men, not of the highest social status although not without means.

Mosslake Fields was a very damp area extending from Hope Street in the west, Crown Street in the east, Oxford Street in the north and Parliament Street in the south and one would expect that most of the 30 lived in or very close to these streets. The exact position of the Cricket Club lay between Chatham Street and Crown Street and was later occupied partly by St. Catherine's church in Abercromby Square. The map on page 8 shows the location of this and subsequent grounds. It is unlikely that they should agree to meet at 6 o'clock in the morning, three times a week if they had long journeys from home to the field itself.

It has always been assumed by the Liverpool C.C. that its progenitor is the Mosslake Club, but there is no firm evidence of this. However, in the Liverpool Record Office there is a small booklet entitled "*The Laws of Cricket as revised by the St. Mary-le-Bone Club 1809*" printed in Liverpool for the use of "L.C.C. established May, 1811."[7] Further evidence of a cricket club calling itself L.C.C. is the **Liverpool Mercury** on October 18th of the same year in a piece of "Original Poetry dedicated to the L.C.C."

> "*On Mersey's banks a town there lies,*
> *Where may be found immense supplies*
> *Of youths both strong and active;*
> *Who like their business passing well,*
> *And yet, if truth historians tell,*
> *Find pleasures more attractive.*

> *These heroes join, and instant dub*
> *Themselves a mighty cricket club,*
> *White hat of scarce four ounces,*
> *A jacket smart, flesh coloured hose,*
> *A cricketer complete compose,*
> *Or my informer bounces."*[8]

Later in the poem, clues are given to the identities of the players, when the writer compares cricket to a lady in such lines as *"'Twas she who made young B . . . to stumble"*. Unfortunately only two of these clues seem to fit in with the list of the 30 gentlemen who formed the Mosslake Club.

Whether the Mosslake Club had by 1811 ceased to exist or had indeed assumed the name of Liverpool C.C. or, the only other possibility, that L.C.C. was a completely new venture, will probably never by known. The newspapers of this period contain no reports of cricket games in Liverpool, nor have I discovered any further mention of local cricket until 1824 when a report of a match is given in the **Liverpool Mercury** of the 21st August. By then the Club was playing at a site in Crabtree Lane (now known as Falkner Street), whence it had moved in 1820. This site had as its boundaries Myrtle, Crown and Falkner Streets. The report is also the first account of Liverpool playing against opposition from outside its own club.[9]

Liverpool v Manchester on ground of the former in Crabtree Lane from 11 till late in the evening.

Liverpool	Manchester
60	50
105	27
165	77

In favour of Liverpool 88.

The Club's stay in Crabtree Lane was a short one and by 1829 they were once again on the move, this time to the Edge Hill district, where they were to remain for over half a century. The first of the Edge Hill grounds was on the south of Wavertree Road beyond Tunnel Road. Next to the ground was a small tavern known as the "Half-Way House", its situation being about half-way between Edge Hill and Wavertree village. This tavern served as a storeroom for kit, changing rooms and committee room as well as providing refreshments both during and after the game. With this move the Club seems to have extended its fixture list playing in addition to Manchester four other clubs on a home and away basis in 1829.[10]

By 1845 the railway network was expanding and the land was required by the Railway Company. The Club was therefore forced to look for alternative accommodation. Apparently the members were groundless during 1846, but by 1847 a suitable site was found in a field situated near Edge Hill Station between Sandy Lane and Spekefield Cottages.

This ground was opened on 22nd May 1847 and a scorebook for part of this season still lies in the committee room at Aigburth. It dates from 7th August of that year and gives details of matches against Manchester and Edge Hill together with two inter-club games. In addition it tells of the first big match played by the Liverpool Club, when 12 of its members strengthened by two professional bowlers, W. Lillywhite and Martingell took on the XI of All England. An early indication of the attitude of the Liverpool C.C. to its professionals, which we shall see lasted well over a century, is indicated in the bowling figures. For Liverpool only the two professionals bowled, Lillywhite's figures being in the 1st innings 39 overs 5 for 41 and in the 2nd 37 overs 6 for 22 and Martingell's 39 overs 5 for 29 and 37 overs 2 for 30. Cricket for the gentlemen meant batting, bowling was hard work and a chore, an activity for which one paid people. Of course once such an idea is established it can become self perpetuating; the professionals are the only ones who bowl, so that both through matches and practice they become more and more proficient at it and the less and less likely is the amateur to be able to compete with them.

The first real opportunity to take stock of the status of the Liverpool Club is provided by the playing records of the 1848 season contained in this same book. By this time it had been in existence for over 40 years. Despite its having had to move on several occasions it could be considered as established. During 1848 it played on 51 occasions, although the majority of these (37) were club games. They had devised numerous different ways of selecting teams for these games, examples of which are Seniors v Juniors, Alphabetical teams, Married v Single, Public Schools v Rest, Volunteers v Non-Volunteers. The other 14 matches were against Birkenhead, Manchester, Cestrian Club of Chester, Olympus, Wrexham and the County of Salop all on a home and away basis plus home games against Rugby School and the Officers of the 46th and 81st Regiments. Most of these games took place mid-week beginning at 11 a.m., ending at 6.30 and lasting two days. The players wore white flannel trousers, linen shirts, tall black hats and their normal day boots.

An unknown writer describing cricket at this ground says

"In those days the ground was reached either by omnibus, cab or railway to Edge Hill Station, then, after jumping over innumerable railway lines, carrying a heavy carpet bag and hurling it over a wall, which had to be climbed, the enthusiastic cricketers arrived at a low rambling structure which served as a pavilion. This was in charge of a man and his wife, who on match days provided a meal, consisting of ponderous joints, beefsteaks, fruit tarts and massive cheeses. One hour was allowed for this meal, but with luck the game was restarted not earlier than 3.15, by which time the younger members of the team had returned from a hasty visit to their respective offices, where after having exhibited an invoice or account sales to their seniors, as proof they had been working, they had jumped into a fly or cab and returned to the ground. On rare occasions a dinner was given to the visitors and the evenings usually closed in singing or even dancing".[11]

Although clearly the Club was a going concern with a quite impressive fixture list, the individual results of the 30 players in that year indicate either their lack of proficiency or more probably the less than perfect nature of the pitches. The highest batting average for 1849 was a mere 15.4 and indeed only 6 of the 30 averaged double figures.[12]

It would seem that this second Edge Hill period of the Club's history is the one which saw great strides made in establishing the Club's importance and its position as part of the recognised social life of the ever growing city.

It is perhaps tempting to look at these events in the context of the Liverpool of the 1840s; of that great, squalid thriving sea port, with its teeming thousands of homeless Irish immigrants, of its filthy cellars and courts, of its cholera, typhus, smallpox and multitudinous other diseases and yet somehow it seems almost an irrelevance. Perhaps it is obscene that it should be so; that up on the hills of Liverpool men could languidly spend their days playing cricket, consuming vast lunches and drinking the night away in pleasant company, whilst no more than a mile away the poor were living and dying in some of the worst slum conditions ever experienced in western civilisation. Yet in reality the only way in which such things impinge on our story is that it was through the poverty of the majority that many of the middle classes became wealthy and turned to such social activities as cricket.

Derek Birley has said of cricket in England during the middle of the 19th century

"In its dream world, cricket, by contrast managed to avoid such harsh instrusions. The industrial revolution in the

LIVERPOOL CRICKET CLUB 1874

Old v Young (Old Team)

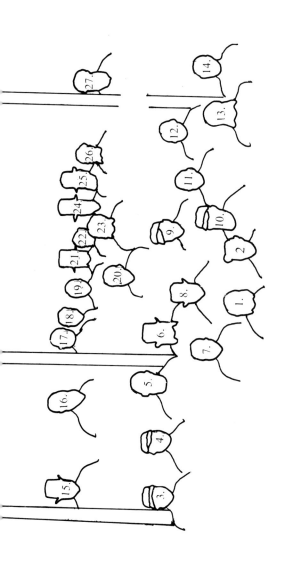

1. C. Todd
2. H.H. Hornby
3. Tranter
4. W. May
5. A. Eccles
6. H.F. Hornby
7. T.D. Hornby
8. Chas Langton
9. F. Napier

10. D. Cunningham
11. D.C. Fraser
12. Wm. Langton
13. W. Todd
14. G. Bromfield
15. Geo Blythe
16. T.R. Stolterfoht
17. E.J. Thornewill
18.

19. Alfred Fletcher
20. W. Horner
21. T.O. Potter
22. Arthur P. Fletcher

24. Arthur Earle
25. D. Carstairs
26. E.W. Rayner
27. W.T. Pears

15

orthodox tradition of cricket literature, is no more than an unpleasant nuisance chewing at the edges of its true values".[13]

By 1859 the standard of the facilities of the Club had improved considerably. In August of that year they were sufficiently established to stage a match between the Gentlemen of the South and the Gentlemen of the North. There was now also a second XI, sometimes so named, sometimes as "an XI" but more often as "Birkett's XI" after the organiser and often the captain of it, J.L. Birkett. The 1st XI that year played 14 fixtures against Birkenhead, Manchester, Western (Eccles), Chester, Warrington, and St. Helens home and away plus Burton, I Zingari, Rossall College and the Bar of the Northern Circuit. The last three are especially interesting for different reasons. I Zingari is probably the most famous of the many amateur wandering clubs of the 19th century and had been in existence since 1845. Some idea of the ethos of I Zingari can be gained by noting the name of the three founders, Sir Spencer Ponsonby-Fane, the Earl of Bessborough and I. Loraine Baldwin and by their use of the term Governor rather than President to describe its leading light.[14] By 1859 it had almost first class status and certainly would not have come to Liverpool had it not expected both good opposition and more importantly the opposition of gentlemen of the right social standing. Similarly the members of the Bar of the Northern Circuit would all consider themselves to be gentlemen. The other fixture given to Rossall College is only one example of the very close and obviously influential ties with the 19th century public schools, ties which were assiduously fostered throughout the century both by invitations to Liverpool and tours by the Club.

It was within the second XI fixtures for 1860 however that a pattern of local Merseyside clubs began to emerge. Here one finds a number of clubs, presumably of lesser status, some of which have gone on to greater prosperity, others which have long since disappeared such as Anfield, Clare Mount and Rock Ferry. Southport and New Brighton were amongst those given 2nd XI status, which is surprising since they could not have been in existence as clubs for more than a couple of years. Other much older clubs such as Ormskirk and Bootle had not as yet been granted a fixture with Liverpool.

Clearly for these young clubs such a fixture at whatever level would have proved to be something of a recognition and would have influenced both the way these clubs were run and the manner in which they played. Even in those clubs which still awaited an invitation, the influence of Liverpool was evident. In the minutes of the first meeting in 1860 of Huyton C.C., "Mr. Eccles was requested to draw up a code of rules to be observed by the 'Huyton C.C.' based on the rules enforced by the 'Liverpool Cricket Club,.'[15]

Whilst these clubs were growing up under the umbrella of Liverpool's influence, the Club itself was developing its own ethos which was to guide it through the next century and continue to be its exemplar through, and despite of, the myriad changes which the city would see. An indication of one of the more pervasive influences has already been seen in the allocation of a 1st XI fixture to Rossall College and Rugby School. It can be seen even more clearly in the introduction from 1866 of an annual public school tour, not of the northern schools, but of the more prestigious ones of the Midlands and south of England. The number of schools played varied from one year to the next; sometimes as few as two, sometimes as many as five. Cheltenham College were played every year up to the 1920s, with more often than not Marlborough, Eton, Clifton, Uppingham and, of course, Rugby also figuring prominently.[16]

Those much quoted feelings expressed by Arthur, Tom Brown's master at Rugby that cricket was more than a game, "it was an institution, the birthright of British boys old and young, as habeas corpus and trial by jury are of British men,"[17] may not be historically accurate, but they are nevertheless part of the mythology of the game, which the public schools above all other bodies helped both to invent and perpetuate.

These noble sentiments, which must have been totally meaningless to most people in the industrial and commercial north west, nevertheless influenced the way in which cricket at Liverpool was played. They would be sustained both by these annual pilgrimages to the public schools and by the introduction into the Club of young men educated at such establishments. The degree to which these ideas became watered down was dependent largely on the numbers of those whose characters had been moulded by them. Indeed it could finally be argued that Liverpool C.C. was allowed to change ultimately and join the rest of the 20th century world as late as the 1960s, largely because this element had for various reasons ceased to exist or be influential there.

Despite the growing importance and influence of the Club it was still powerless against the wheels of commerce when once again the railway needed to expand in 1877. This event does, however, underline how influential the members of the Club were. No less a person than the Earl of Sefton came to their aid and allowed the club the use of his grounds at Croxteth Hall for many of their matches, although the members practiced at less exalted sites within the city, even travelling as far as Birkenhead. There is no record of the Earl playing cricket himself, although his interest went further than merely providing facilities. On occasions during the 1880s he appeared as President at committee meetings.[18]

This use of the Croxteth Hall grounds continued for three years but it was always seen as a temporary measure. By 1880 plans were well advanced to acquire what was to prove the club's finest and final home at Aigburth or Grassendale as the precise area was then called.

The Liverpool and South West Lancashire Cricket Ground Co. Ltd. was formed to buy the land. Each share cost £25 and £15,000 was raised both to purchase the land and build the pavilion. Nowhere is there more striking evidence of the esteem which Liverpool C.C. had by then, in the city, for the list of shareholders read like a Who's Who of Victorian Liverpool.[19]* The company was not purely a philanthropic one; it expected in time to make a profit whilst providing the best possible facilities for sport and primarily for cricket. From a letter read to the committee in June 1885 containing minor alterations to the lease, the Club had to pay a minimum rent of £200 per annum, £100 of which had to be paid by the 1st August. This was met by 10 shillings of each member's £2.2/- annual subscription automatically going to the Company. The Company was also entitled to 25% of any gate money without its being liable for any loss which might be made there.[20] The Ground Company still exists today although its shares were bought at their face value by the Club after the Second World War and are now controlled by three trustees appointed by the Club.

Costs in these early days at Aigburth were of course very high. Apart from the building of the magnificent pavilion by Cubitts which still stands today, there was in the years 1882-3 almost £1000 spent on improving the ground. £459 of this came from a loan from the Bank of Liverpool, £250 from the company and £281 in loans and donations from 173 different members.

It is clear that the Company and the Cricket Club, despite many of the shareholders also being members, were by no means one and the same thing. In 1887 a covered stand had been built at a cost of £200 with money loaned by the Company. The intention seems to have been to charge admission to the stand and for three-quarters of the receipts (less the cost of collection) to go to pay off the Company's loan. Thereafter the Company would receive a quarter of the receipts. A dispute arose as to whether members should have to pay this admission charge. A letter from the Company makes clear their intention:

". . . as the free admission of members would seriously curtail and indeed, owing to their number, might absolutely put an end to the earning power of the stand, the Directors of the Company consider that members should be charged for admission . . . and that their free admission would be distinctly contrary to the original intention".[21]

From the very beginning at Aigburth it was clearly no longer simply a club for gentlemen interested in playing cricket. It was a business which was to grow rapidly year by year. In 1883 there were over 600 members, of whom no more than 45 actually played cricket. A full time secretary was employed at a salary of £200. Five 'ground bowlers' (professionals) were engaged "at £3 per week each for the months of May, June, July and August."[22] Strangely the five, Bowley, White, Richards and William and Alfred Price, all came from Nottinghamshire County Club. As their title suggests they were employed primarily to act as bowlers for the members at practice, but they were also expected to help on the ground. A full time groundsman G. Ubsdell worked probably most of his time on the square and practice wickets. Ubsdell appears to have been paid about £3 a week, but was permanent being employed for the whole year. Simply because he was so seldom mentioned in the minutes, he appears to have been a very satisfactory employee and this is confirmed by his being granted a quite substantial wage increase in May 1889 of seven shillings a week.[23]

Most of the other Merseyside clubs at this time employed only one professional. Very often he was chosen as much for his ability to bolster up the team as for his coaching and bowling ability. Such does not appear necessarily to have been the case at Liverpool. Indeed there seems to have been some resentment expressed by the members of the professionals playing and thereby presumably taking the place of a member who had paid his subscription. Throughout the 1880s there was considerable debate, as to whether fixtures especially local ones, should be club ones or club and ground, by which was meant whether the teams should consist solely of members or not. A resolution of January 3rd 1884 decided "that all local matches are to be arranged Club and Ground with the exception of Birkenhead and Sefton Park which are to be Club only." The idea presumably was that the more prestigious games should be for amateurs only. However, this does not seem to have solved the problem for in April the opinion of the General Committee was that "it is not binding on the Match Committee, in the exercise of their discretion, to play Professionals in local matches." The following year it was decided to print all the fixtures "as if club only would be played against local clubs, but at the same time the Committee reserved the right to play ground if necessary."[24]

The committee in attempting to arrive at a solution to the problem was obviously under pressure from different sources. Whilst the playing members may have resented their own non-selection, the professionals saw in playing a respite from the harder physical work on the ground, an opportunity to enhance their reputations and thus their earning power and also the chance of making a bit of extra money in expenses.

These match expenses themselves became another bone of contention and may have prejudiced the committee against selecting the professionals. As early as 1883 it was decided, presumably after the professionals had been taking advantage of the system

> "that the ground bowlers should have dinner provided at the Expense of the Club, only when the matches began at a time when an interval for Luncheon was deemed necessary. At all other times, those who were actively engaged in the match were to leave their work early to have dinner and get back on the ground in time for the commencement of the match. As this did not appear to have been understood by the ground bowlers, the following claims for dinner money were allowed".[25]

These claims varied from 7/6 to 2/6 presumably at 2/6 a day.

Such practices probably went on all the time, being checked occasionally when they became excessive, as presumably they had done by May 1889.

> "The professionals' match expenses were brought before the committee by the secretary who considered them to be very excessive and it was resolved that when away from home 2/- each be allowed for Tea and refreshments and on whole day matches the Captain pay for their dinners and the Professionals were also informed that the porterage charges must be considerably reduced. With regard to the loss of practice balls . . . recommended that each Professional should have 6 balls and to account for them to Ubsdell at the end of each day."[26]

The other source of pressure on the committee probably came from the mass of club members who would be divided in their desire for the Club to perform well, which they were more likely to do with the assistance of the professionals and a wish for the game to be played by amateurs in the true amateur spirit.

Prior to 1887 the catering had been leased out to the licensee of the Aigburth Hotel for £25 a season. Either he had proved unsatisfactory or he was unable to cope with the growing demand. Whatever the reason, in 1887 it was considered necessary to employ a full time steward and a Mr. Flay was engaged who had previously been in the employment of the Honorary Treasurer, Mr. G.C.H. Dunlop.[27] So by 1887, the Liverpool Cricket Club with 850 members had a staff, in the playing season, of at least 8, a secretary, a steward, a groundsman (plus occasional assistants) and 5 professionals.

The decisions on staffing the pavilion and ground lay very much under the control of a handful of men who formed the General Committee. The size of this committee varied from year to year, but seems to have been comprised of between 12 and 15 members.

There is little doubt that the 15 who served as committee members in 1882 were men of considerable means and held positions of influence in the city.

Only two cannot be traced through the Directory of that year. The others are listed below with both their occupations and home addresses. The latter were largely either in the city or in that growing residential area around Princes and Sefton Parks.[28]

George C. Dunlop — Cotton Broker — 13, Rumford Street,
Thomas Hornby J.P. — Merchant — Olive Mount, Mill Lane,
  Wavertree.
John F. Collier Esq. — Judge of County Court —
  45, Canning Street.
Danson Cunningham — Cotton Broker — 31, Falkner Sq.
Charles Langton Esq., J.P. — Bark Hill, Aigburth.
William H. Porter — Shipbuilder — Blundell Sands.
Henry B. Parr — Stock and Share Broker — Rodney Street.
Arthur Maples — Wine Merchant — Peel Street, Toxteth Park.
Arthur Isaacson — Merchant — 76, Huskisson Street.
Edward Roper — Gentleman — 43, Kingsley Road. (some doubt)
A.J. Steel — Shipowner — 2, South Hill Grove, St. Michaels.
D.Q. Steel — Solicitor — 28, Greenheys Road, Princes Park.
E. Kewley
P.J. McCullogh   not listed in 1882 Gore' Directory
George Bird — Merchant — Grange Lodge, Gateacre.

There were seldom more than 5 or 6 who attended any given committee meeting, the venue for which varied depending on the time of year. In the summer months they took place at 5 o'clock in the evening in the Committee Room in the pavilion, but in the winter there seemed to be no set time or place. Generally they were held at the offices in the city of one of the committee members. The times at which they were held also varied but as a general rule were around 2 o'clock in the afternoon on a day presumably mutually acceptable.

This would suggest firstly that most of the committee either worked in the city or lived close enough to be able to attend and secondly that they were in a sufficiently elevated position in their firms to enable them to take time off in mid-afternoon to attend to the affairs of a cricket club.

These early minutes tell us much about the problems of the Club and the decisions which the committee came to, but they give little indication of the way in which the meetings were conducted and the type of personalities who formed the committee, whether they worked hard at the job or whether it was more of a "divertissement" and a useful social prop to be associated with the Club. It does seem however, that the committee members ran the Club as a pastime. The irregularity with which most of them attended meetings, reflected the seriousness with which they viewed their duties. But, of course, it did work; they merely needed to keep a hand on the rudder, to steer the Club along the right lines. Little more was required. Any problems could easily be solved by the affluence of the members, by the ease with which they could raise loans and through the assistance of the Land Company.

Not only were they financially secure in the last years of the 19th century, but they were also immeasurably stronger than any other club for miles around. So strong in fact that in the 1880s they fielded two 1st XI sides each Saturday. Their most famous player was A.G. Steel, the most illustrious of the five brothers who all played for Lancashire and arguably the best cricketer ever to come from Merseyside. A.G. like W.G. Grace, was known by his initials and at the height of his fame, no England team was complete without him. He holds a record in English cricket when at the age of 19 in 1878, he headed the English bowling averages taking 164 wickets for 9.40 each. He was also a splendid batsman, who scored 148 against the Australians at Lords in 1884 and captained England on three occasions.

From the time of its acquisition of the Aigburth ground, Liverpool has always staged at least one county game, not quite as of right, for there have been several attempts by the Manchester club at Old Trafford to have all the county matches played there. [29] Possibly even more interesting are the matches played by Liverpool and District against other counties and touring sides. [30] These show that almost a century before the planners conceived the idea of Merseyside as a county, as far as cricket was concerned the Liverpool gentlemen felt themselves to be strong enough to act as one. The first of these matches was against the 1882 Australians, although strictly speaking, despite its billing as a Liverpool and District XI there were 5 professionals including the famous R.E. Barlow drafted in from Manchester. By 1886 however, the side put out against the Australians was truly representative of Merseyside with H.B., A.G., and D.Q. Steel, E.C. Hornby and J. White from Liverpool, C. Holden and E. Smith from Birkenhead Park, C. Shore, T. Evans and E. Ratcliffe from Sefton and P. Dobell from Huyton. The report of the match suggests that in all probability the Liverpool side would have won had it not been for a solitary effort by the Australian H.J.H. Scott who scored 80 out of a second innings total of 141 for 8 to secure a draw, the Australians having been dismissed in their first innings for 152.

Details of these 'first class' matches of the Liverpool and District XI were collected by George Brooking a local cricket correspondent and fanatic, and a copy resides in the Aigburth pavilion. Apart from the Australians other tourists included the South Africans (1894 - 1904), the West Indies (1900), Canada (1887 and 1910), the Philadelphians (1884 - 1911) and the Parsees (1888). Other opponents were Oxford University, Cambridge University against whom they played 15 times from 1894 - 1920 and the counties of Nottinghamshire (1889), Somerset (1903), Yorkshire 8 matches between 1887 - 95 and Gloucestershire (1901 - 2). Of the 8 matches against the full Yorkshire XI,[31] four were won by Liverpool. With the Gloucestershire side came the mighty hitter Jessop, who in one innings compiled 140 out of 174 in 90 minutes. "From E.C. Hornby's bowling he hit 17 in one over, including one terrific drive on to the pavilion verandah, just missing the clock." No one nowadays can remember a hit carrying anywhere near this distance and it is a ground which has seen the best of the modern day hitters such as Botham and Clive Lloyd

In most of these games Liverpool C.C. provided at least half the players. Clearly were they to have fielded their full 1st XI they would have been far too powerful for the local Merseyside opposition in these last years of the 19th century. Only Birkenhead Park could ever seriously challenge them. In the 23 games between the two clubs from the first match at Aigburth in 1881 up to 1896, 18 were drawn, 4 won by Liverpool and one, in 1886, won by Park, although on that day Liverpool were without the services of E.C.Hornby and three of the four Steel brothers.[32]

In considering the problem of finding suitably strong opposition, it is opportune to pause and examine the club's fixture list in the 1880s. As has already been mentioned, the club felt itself strong enough to put out two 1st XI's, but this must have created more selection problems than it solved and at the end of the 1887 season it was decided that "one first team match and an 'A' team match be played on Saturdays in future instead of two first team." As a result of this the following matches were arranged for the season 1888. [33]

Saturday 1st XI matches —
Birkenhead Park (2), Sefton (2), Huyton (2), Rock Ferry (2), Preston (2), Warrington (2), Werneth, Wigan, Bolton and Boughton Hall (1 away and a weekday match at home), Northern, Bootle, New

Aigburth in 1894 – on the occasion of Northern Lawn Tennis Tournament.

Brighton and Dingle (1 on Saturday and a two evenings match) and Western (Eccles) and Leyland (1 match each).

The 1st XI played on 22 Saturdays, whereas the 'A' team's matches for some reason were played up to the end of July.

Saturday 'A' team matches —

Stoneycroft (2), Birkenhead Victoria (2), Prescot (2), Oxton (2), Stanley (2), Broad Green (1), West Derby (1), Southport Alexandra (1), H.M. Customs (1), Liverpool Police (1), Liverpool Challenge Cup Winner (1), Formby (2).

Week-day 1st XI matches —

Rossall (one day), Uppingham (2 days), School Trip Week, Warwick (2 days), Manchester (one day), Grange (2 days), West of Scotland (2 days) Free Foresters (2 days), Uppingham Rovers (2 days), Hoi Pepnbeumenoi (2 days), Old Cheltonians (2 days), and Australia and Yorkshire (against Liverpool and District XI's).

Of the clubs which ultimately became the Liverpool Competition, Birkenhead Park, Sefton, Huyton, Boughton Hall, Northern, Bootle and New Brighton had already been granted 1st XI status, whilst Oxton, Formby and Southport were accorded 'A' XI games. So by 1888 the majority had contacts with Liverpool and one would imagine that for all of them their seasons would be complete if they beat the mighty Liverpool or even avoided defeat. For Liverpool, however, one had the feeling that these matches were of far less significance than those against say the Public Schools or the Free Foresters.

We have, as we enter the 20th century, a picture of a Club arrogant in its self confidence, as well it might be. A Club, not only possessing the finest players, the wealthiest members, but also facilities incomparably superior to those of any of the other local clubs and serving as an example and a guide to all these smaller clubs around it.

REFERENCES

1. C. Brookes, *English Cricket* (Weidenfeld & Nicholson 1978), p.3.
2. From — *"A Sketch of Liverpool Cricket Club."* Author unknown. (1930). p.1.
3. An *original broadsheet* found in an old scorebook at Aigburth. (Printed 1807).
4. R. Bowen, *Cricket: A History of its Growth and Development throughout the World* (Eyre & Spottiswood 1970), p.264.
5. Gore, Johnson, *The Liverpool directory* (Liverpool 1807).
6. Gore, Johnson, *Directory of Liverpool and its environs* (Liverpool 1818).
7. Liverpool Record Office H 796.3506.
8. *Liverpool Mercury* October 18th 1811.
9. *A Sketch of Liverpool C.C.* op. cit. p.2.

10. Ibid. p.2.
11. Ibid, p.2-3.
12. Scorebook 1847-9. Held by Liverpool C.C.
13. D. Birley, *The Willow Wand* (MacDonald & James 1979). p.8.
14. E.W. Swanton, *Follow on* (Fontana 1978), p.46.
15. Minute Book of Huyton C.C. Committee meeting 7th May 1860. Deposited at Huyton Library.
16. *L.C.C. Public School Tour.* Volume 1. 1866-1896. Volume II 1897-1924. These booklets were printed some time in the 1920s editor and publisher unknown. A few copies are held at Aigburth.
17. Thomas Hughes, *Tom Brown's School Days.* (1857) p.301.
18. As for example May 7th 1883. Minute Book of the General Committee of Liverpool Cricket Club.
19. From the Liverpool and South West Lancashire Cricket Ground Co. Ltd.'s allotment book held by Liverpool C.C. Among the 150 shareholders can be found such names as Brocklebank, Crosfield, Tate, Langton, Holt and Napier as well as the Earls of Derby, Sefton and Latham.
20. Minute Book L.C.C. op. cit. June 3rd. 1885.
21. Ibid. March 28th 1887.
22. Ibid. August 8th 1884.
23. Ibid. May 9th 1889.
24. Ibid. March 24th 1885.
25. Ibid. June 20th 1883.
26. Ibid. May 27th 1889.
27. Ibid. April 25th 1887.
28. *Gore's Directory of Liverpool and its environs* (Liverpool 1881).
29. *Lancashire County and Manchester Cricket Club.* Report of its annual meeting given in the Liverpool Mercury January 25th 1883.
30. G.A. Brooking (ed), *The Complete History of Liverpool and District versus Colonial and Foreign Teams, First Class Counties and Cambridge University.* (T.W. Gornall, Liverpool 1931).
31. Yorkshire at the time were led by Lord Hawke whose team it was said consisted of nine drunks and a chapel parson. This did not however prevent them from winning the county championship in 1893, 1894 and 1898.
32. Scorebook for 1886. Held at Aigburth.
33. Minute Book L.C.C. op. cit. September 23rd. 1887.

CHAPTER TWO

150 years old — Bootle and Ormskirk

Liverpool apart, only two of the Competition clubs have a history which predates the railway network reaching their area. As in so many other aspects of English life, the coming of the railways was a significant factor in the development of cricket. Most directly, they made it possible for clubs to improve greatly their fixture lists and thereby their own standards. But the railways also led to the growth of suburbia and the creation of dormitory towns and seaside resorts. The middle class merchants and professional people, who, as we have seen already, were more often than not the prime movers in establishing cricket clubs, moved into these desirable residential areas vacating the immediate outskirts of the city where they had earlier lived. This outwards movement can similarly be seen in Liverpool C.C.'s travels to its eventual home in the affluent suburb of Aigburth.

Bootle Cricket Club.

Bootle C.C., one of the three formed before the great social changes created by the railways, now lies well inside the industrial sprawl of Liverpool dockland. Yet in its early days it would have been populated by those very people who later moved with the railways northwards along the Southport line. The Club has long recognised its founding as being 1833, and their 150th anniversary was celebrated recently in 1983. This is, however, based on rather tenuous evidence. H.S. Brown, who wrote a brief, unpublished history of the Club, quotes from an article in the **Bootle Times** of 1935 which was itself a reprint from the **Bootle Times** of 1883.

> "For upwards of fifty years it (the Club) has held under Lord Derby the ground on Irlam Road on which so many famous matches have been played, and there is said to have been in existence a letter written by the late Earl of Derby, promising that as long as there were eleven men in Bootle to play cricket the Club should never be dismissed from the ground."[1]

Of course it matters little that 1833 may not be the correct date, almost certainly it was about that time, but it does shed an interesting light on how such claims are made.

James Sherriff's map of "the Environs of Liverpool" in 1829 gives some idea of how different Bootle must have been in those days.

Northwards from Liverpool the docks and concomitant urbanisation extended no further than the recent Irish Ferry Terminals. Bootle Township and its cricket ground, when it came into being, lay 2 ½ miles away in still largely rural surroundings. It had however begun to change, taking on the appearance of a seaside resort. It had

"a charming situation for visitors. In the months of July, August and early September, the beach is covered with immense numbers of people employing a number of caravans to conduct them into the water. Writers and artists came to Bootle to refresh their minds and gather inspiration."[2]

Although its life as a seaside resort was shortlived, again because of the railways providing access to even more suitable places, the building of huge mansions and villas by the professional men of Liverpool had a more lasting impact. The Bootle of 1850 was described by Sir William B. Forwood with its "houses of importance surrounded by park-like grounds." His reminiscences also enable us to pinpoint fairly accurately the site of the early cricket ground.

"Going northwards (along Derby Road) we had several large residences including Durham Hall, a house of much importance; then came the Toll Bar with Bootle Cricket Ground beyond."[3]

Nowadays the Fire Station occupies this site which is bounded by Derby, Atlantic, Irlam and Strand Roads.

No club records exist before 1882 and nothing at all before 1846. In that year there is a reference to Bootle playing the newly formed Birkenhead Park in that Club's early fixture list, but no other details.[4] More concrete evidence of these early matches can be found, surprisingly, in the Museum at Lords, where there is a mounted ball on which, in gold lettering, is ;the inscription, "Won by Bootle Cricket Club from Lord Stanley's Cricket Club at Knowsley Hall 14 Sep 1858 with 10 wickets to fall."[5] Although this tells us little about the standard of the Bootle Club, not knowing the strength of his Lordship's team, it does tell us something about their standing. It seems highly unlikely that a team of working class Bootle people would ever have been invited to play such a fixture.

It is also dangerous to overestimate the importance of a match in 1865 against an All-England XI. The All-England matches were very much business ventures. As long as a club could guarantee a profit either by gate money or donation, the All-England side would play virtually anywhere. First founded in 1846 by William Clarke, a professional, it predates the formation of county cricket clubs and was the first attempt by professionals to break away from the system of patronage by which they had previously been employed. "They were first and foremost money making businesses, but they also spread knowledge of the game and intensified enthusiasm for it."[6]

As time passed and the interest in county matches increased they attracted less and less support and ceased to exist after 1869. By the time they came to Bootle they were very much on the wane and probably even more prepared to accept a fixture anywhere. Despite this they were far too good for the 22 of Bootle who were dismissed for 58, none of them reaching double figures. The Eleven had little trouble in passing this total and among their hits was "one into the refreshment booth, a gentleman being somewhat staggered by having a glass knocked out of his hand."[7]

Whatever the standing of the All-England XI may have been in the country as a whole, its arrival in these small northern towns, still rather untutored and remote in cricketing terms, must have been an occasion for celebration. When they visited Runcorn the local paper announcing the game added,

> "the band of the 7th Cheshire Rifle Volunteers has been engaged to play throughout the afternoon and it is expected that the ground will be visited by a numerous and elite assemblage."[8]

The visits of the All-England XI may not have been particularly unique ones, but there is no doubt about the next big occasion at Bootle. In 1868 the first tour of England was undertaken by Australians. Strangely the team was comprised of black Australians and possibly even more strangely they had fixtures against Bootle. How these came to be organised is not known, but most probably it was through a contact with the team manager, an English professional living in Australia named Charles Lawrence. The matches were played over three days. The first was won by the aborigines by 9 wickets and the second just as convincingly by 154 runs. The scoresheet of this second encounter is worth reprinting if only for the extraordinary names of the participants.

Aboriginal Cricketers – 1868.

ABORIGINES
First Innings

Lawrence	b Randon	1
Bullockey	run out	2
Tiger	b Clegg	13
Mullagh	c Taylor b Benson	51
Redcap	b Benson	21
Cuzens	b Benson	8
Twopenny	b Benson	4
Peter	b Court	30
Charley	b Court	12
Dick-a-Dick	b Court	0
Mosquito	not out	1
	Extras	5
	Total	148

Second Innings

Lawrence	lbw b Sharpe	22
Bullockey	c Taylor b Sharpe	0
Tiger	c and b Benson	11
Mullagh	lbw b Sharpe	78
Redcap	c Gibbons b Sharpe	1
Cuzens	b Clegg	28
Twopenny	c Chesworth b Sharpe	6
Peter	lbw Sharpe	1
Charley	run out	2
Dick-a-Dick	b Sharpe	1
Mosquito	not out	0
	Extras	6
	Total	156

BOOTLE
First Innings

Nicholson	c Cuzens b Mullagh	12
Taylor	b Mullagh	3
Hampshire	c Bullockey B Mullagh	0
Jervis	b Lawrence	10
Benson	c Bullockey b Mullagh	3
Chesworth	b Mullagh	17
Gibbons	c Bullockey b Lawrence	0
Garrow	st Mullagh b Lawrence	20
Sharpe	c Redcap b Mullagh	18
Court, jun	not out	4
Clegg	c Bullockey b Mullagh	3
	Extras	1
	Total	91

Second Innings

Nicholson	c and b Lawrence	11
Taylor	b Mullagh	0
Hampshire	b Lawrence	15
Jervis	b Mullagh	6
Benson	c Charley b Lawrence	2
Chesworth	b Lawrence	12
Gibbons	b Mullagh	0
Garrow	not out	0
Sharpe	c Bullockey b Mullagh	1
Court, jun	run out	7
Clegg	b Lawrence	0
	Extras	5
	Total	59

The matches attracted huge crowds not so much, one imagines, out of any love of cricket, as for the novelty of the occasion and for the exhibitions the Aborigines staged in addition. These consisted of such items as throwing the boomerang, spear and an implement called a waddy, a thin stick with a large knob which was made to skim along the ground. The high spot of the exhibition, according to one journalist was when

"Dick-a-Dick armed with a shield next went through his feat of eluding a constant fire of cricket balls, thrown at him from a distance of seven or eight yards, and the rapidity with which he escaped some of the shots by a twist of his body, the dexterity with which he parried those which were aimed straight at his person, made the exhibition one of the most exciting features of the programme."

He concludes dismissively that

"the remaining events proved devoid of interest and the performances concluded with a second shower of boomerangs."[9]

One spectator certainly did not find this part of the exhibition 'devoid of interest', as a news item in a national newspaper recorded,

" . . . a boomerang thrown by Mullagh was carried by the wind among the audience. It struck a gentleman on the head, the brim of his hat saving the face from severe laceration. As it was the boomerang cut through the hat and inflicted a severe wound across the brow. Surgical aid was at once procured and the gentleman was able to return home."[10]

Mullagh must indeed have been a fine sportsman. Top scorer in both innings, eleven wickets and a stumping not to mention the laying out of spectators.

By the 1880s the old predominantly residential nature of Bootle had gone for ever. The population, which in 1851 had numbered only just over 4,000, was by then over 27,000 and increasing ever more rapidly. By the turn of the century it reached the 60,000 mark. The docks had taken over the one time seaside resort and the commercial value of the immediate hinterland had spiralled. Despite the late Earl of Derby's promise of cricket in perpetuity at Irlam Road, his son was rather more realistic.

In July 1882 the Club was given notice to quit. The following year, this notice having expired, it was offered a 25 acre site in Hawthorn Road on a 14 year lease. This was obviously too large for just a cricket club and well beyond the members means, but the terms were felt to be so favourable that they came to an agreement with the Town Council. By this, the Council acquired all the land to use as a public recreation ground and the Club became its tenants for that piece required for cricket.[11]

It is interesting to examine, in a little more detail, this arrangement and the way in which the Club raised the money for a pavilion and ground preparation. Unlike the Southport, New Brighton and Liverpool clubs the members had chosen not to form themselves into a company. It seems unlikely that such a course of action did not occur to them, as the other three clubs all formed their companies at more or less the same time as Bootle were moving.

The most important point is therefore that the club chose not to own its land. In the short term this was beneficial as the council bore the cost of land purchase. In the longer term it would always remain a tenant, limited in the improvements and changes which could be made and perhaps more disastrously, unable effectively to enclose its land. Hence the vandalism, to which the situation in a public park has always made it susceptible. This vandalism is no result of the post-war Welfare State, as many social observers would have us believe. H.S. Brown whose career with the club began before the First World War talked in 1942 of the

> "damage through the depredation of the youths of the district through breaking into the Pavilion and damaging all the fittings. We can usually expect to pay £30 or £40 every year on this account."[12]

This view is reinforced by a newspaper article in 1946.

> "After running without interruption for 113 years, through several minor wars and two world wars and surviving all the German bombing, Bootle Cricket Club may be forced to close

down through the wilful damage and destruction of its own townfolk."

In addition to the extensive damage which the Club was forced to repair when it regained possession after the war, there were, in the last week of July 1946 alone, four burglaries in five nights. The bowling pavilion, which lay behind the cricket ground, had been in excellent condition before the war. By 1946 it had disappeared completely having been removed plank by plank.[13]

If the ground had not been situated in a public park, this would not necessarily have prevented vandalism, but the Club would have been in a much stronger position to provide deterrents. If only for this reason, the original decision in 1884 seems, in hindsight, to have been the wrong one. It is however an understandable one, when one considers the cost. For less than £1,400 Southport bought their land, levelled it and built a pavilion. In comparison Bootle required that much just to prepare the ground and build a pavilion. The arrangement with the Council must have seemed, at the time, a very welcome expediency.

In raising this money the Club initially asked for public subscriptions. Some idea of the standing of the Club in the eyes of the Bootle public can be seen in the response to the appeal. By the time of the Bootle Times article in 1883 "upwards of £420" had already been received. Additionally a mortgage of £5,000 was obtained, but this still left it about £500 short.[14]

A small notebook, bound in black leather, in the Club's possession, tells the story of how this sum was raised. It details the affairs of the Bazaar Committee which met regularly from 31st July 1883 until 9th January of the following year, when its members resolved "that the balance of £516-4-11 from Bazaar Account, be handed over to the Funds of the Bootle Cricket Club."

The list of patrons of this venture is impressive. Lord Derby, two M.P.s, the Mayor and no less than 15 J.P.s. Derby, however, obviously did not wish to involve himself other than as a figurehead and "could not accede to the wish of the committee", which was for him to formally open the bazaar on the 13th December, and this duty fell to the Mayor. It was a very tasteful affair, akin to the church fetes of today, although one patron wrote to the committee "complaining of Raffles at Bazaar and refusing to allow his name to be used if such was the case." Beer and spirits, it had very early on been decided, should be banned.

The handsome profit was made by a combination of stalls selling goods which had been donated, various entertainments and side shows and an admission fee of 1/- a day. The musical entertainment was provided by Mr. Karl Meyder's band "playing under his personal conductorship" for a fee of £25. The minutes of the Bazaar Committee end with the comment from the secretary.

"Here endeth the First Lesson. May the next man learn the Second better."[15]

Not all the affairs of the 19th century Bootle Cricket Club were conducted in so decorous a manner. Indeed the activities of one of the Bazaar Committee members gives lie to the view that cricket in those days was a less boisterous and an altogether more traditional and sporting business.

Eighteen years before the bazaar, one of its luminaries, a Mr. G.T. Raine had been involved in some hybrid cricket games when as "a distinguished member of the Bootle Cricket Club", he had challenged "Mr. W. Langley of the Atlas C.C." to a single wicket match. Although neither were particularly talented cricketers, the match seems to have engendered a good deal of interest and of money changing hands.

"Mr. Raine won the toss for choice of innings and elected to go in, but he did not stay long, being bowled the second ball amidst great applause from Mr. Langley's admirers. In a few minutes the colossal form of Mr. Langley was seen at the wickets and soon got down to work making some very fine hits which his opponent should have made him run instead of giving him so many for the hit, as it was evident Mr. Langley had not trained for this match. He scored 8 and was well bowled by the twenty seventh ball, which with a wide increased his total to 9. After a short interval, Mr. Raine commenced his second innings. He had a very narrow escape the first ball bowled, the second he hit for 1 and the third he was clean bowled, to the evident great glee of his opponents and the deep sympathy of his numerous friends."[16]

The sequel to this unhappy episode in G.T. Raine's career came in the form of an advertisement in the "**Mercury**" "Reward £5 — strayed from his Home, a well known single-wicket player." Whether he had imbibed too deeply after his disappointment or simply wished to avoid "the deep sympathy of his numerous friends", who had invested money on him remains unknown.[17]

Gambling had always played an integral part in the development of English cricket in the 18th and 19th centuries. Indeed the early laws of the game were constructed specifically to enable gambling debts on the matches to be paid. Many of the 18th century teams belonging to wealthy members of the landed gentry played for wagers often as much as 1000 guineas and not unnaturally side bets were laid between the supporters of these teams. As late as the 1880s the laws of the game as printed in a scorebook of the time, have a section headed 'Bets' which clearly lays down the circumstances under which bets are to be paid.[18]

Another reminder of the boisterous nature of 19th century Bootle cricket was given in an article in **"The Porcupine"** and headed, "Fast Bowling at Bootle."

"The Bootle Cricketers and Bowlers have recently dined. Porcupine does not consider the mere fact of their dining as a astonishingly extraordinary fact; but it appears that the Bootle 'Luffey' and 'Struggles' suffered from superfluous excitement consequent on the meal. Not content with the one day's 'flare up', they were discovered bowling on the following afternoon and still hankering after the 'cup' . . . it would be well if the Bootle 'flannels' would be so good as to moderate their transports and work off their spirits in a less vociferous manner."[19]

The move to new premises and the building of a fine pavilion seems to have pushed Bootle into the top flight of Merseyside clubs. Indeed in its first season at Wadham Road (as the club's address now is), the team lost on only three occasions, on two of which Sefton were the opponents. Included in the many victories was a Club and Ground game against Liverpool at Aigburth. There seems little doubt that this was a win over a full Liverpool side, as the home team used 4 of their 5 professionals.[20]

It is perhaps appropriate to examine how Bootle C.C. stood relative to its mighty neighbour. The accounts of the two clubs in the 1880s give a good indication of this. The overall expenditure on the day to day running of the club at Liverpool in 1883 was £1511; at Bootle it was £380. The wages bill at Aigburth was £674 and at Bootle £195. Liverpool had 600 members whose subscriptions and entrance fees amounted to £1,322, whereas only £399 was collected in subscriptions at Bootle.[21] It would seem that Bootle may have 'arrived', in so far as it had become a cricketing power to reckon with in the area, but that it was in comparison with its wealthy neighbour still a second-rate club. Moreover, situated where it was, a cricket club in a park in an area which had already seen better days, things were unlikely to get easier. Bootle C.C. did have many periods when its cricketers were extremely successful, but as a club it was to become increasingly an oasis in an ever more depressing landscape.

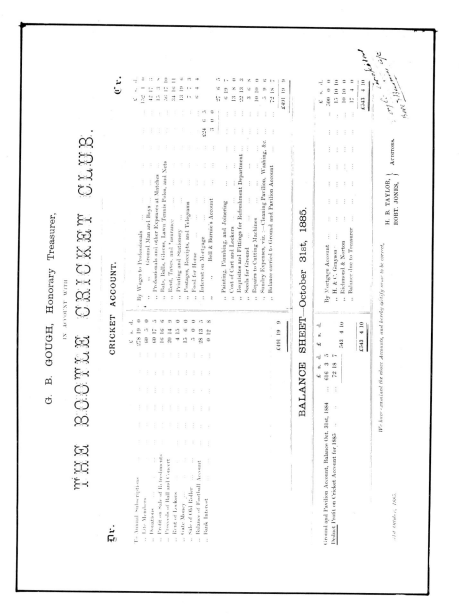

The Bootle Cricket Club Accounts Sheet.

Ormskirk Cricket Club

Ormskirk is the other club which predates the railways network reaching its area, but its longevity is one of the few ways in which its development bears any resemblance to that of Bootle.

Geographically Ormskirk is much closer to Liverpool than is Southport, which despite the protests of many of its inhabitants is today firmly settled administratively in Merseyside. Yet despite its leavening of ex-Liverpool residents, Ormskirk remains avowedly Lancastrian. Its accent is Lancashire as are its pace of life and traditions.

It lies, as do Southport, St. Helens and Chester on the perimeter of the Liverpool Competition and its development like that of these other clubs owes something to the influence of towns and clubs outside the area.

Ormskirk is, as it has been for centuries, a centre, a market town both for townships surrounding it, Halsall, Scarisbrick, Parbold, Newburgh, Skelmersdale and Aughton and the many other smaller settlements and farms. It thus has an identity of its own, a quality which is uniquely Ormskirk. Of all the towns with cricket clubs in the Liverpool Competition it appears to have changed the least over the past hundred years.

Ormskirk C.C. claims to date back to 1835, but I have been unable to find direct evidence of this. There are a number of newspaper articles written this century which state that this is so, but none of the writers indicate how they have acquired this knowledge. In all probability they are based on a short history of the club written in 1935 by Walter Stretch who had been the Hon. Secretary for over 50 years. This history was based on minute books and other club records, but in his opening paragraph, he admits that

> "there is little to say of the first 20 years, as no records are available, but the cricket field was then in Ruff Lane and the game was generally played in the evenings and on holidays as there was no Saturday half holiday in those days."[22]

It is of course possible that no records were kept, and that the affairs of the club were conducted on a casual ad hoc basis. Considering, however, the penchant for cricketers to compile records, this seems unlikely and probably as with so many other clubs, they were simply not looked after and have disappeared for ever.

Some of the later 19th century records have survived, and the story of their rescue could perhaps explain why so much has disappeared. Although established clubs realised the necessity of recording their meetings, scores and so on, there was not, understandably, the awareness of the value and interest of these records to future generations. This is not solely a 19th century failing. The Ormskirk secretary of the time tells how the existing records were saved from the pyrogenic intentions of a well-meaning employee. It illustrates vividly how all historical evidence is often purely a matter of chance.

> "Quite recently (about 10 years ago) the groundsman decided to clear out the cellars, in which there were a number of tea chests with old scorebooks, photos and things that had been taken down and needed renovation and things that were in his eyes really junk. Having a good deal of initiative and not always a good lot of common sense he decided one day, that he'd have a nice bonfire. It was only just by chance that I arrived at the time but most of the damage was done. I managed to save the minute books but the photos and scorebooks had all gone."[23]

One can readily imagine that similar incidents must have occurred on countless occasions and not just in Ormskirk or in cricket clubs.

The local "**Ormskirk Advertiser**" was first printed in the 1850's. Local newspapers are invariably the best source and it is here in 1853 that one finds the first record of the Ormskirk C.C. playing a match against Southport in which Lord Skelmersdale, later Earl of Lathom, made 7 runs.[24] Exactly where the Southport team came from is rather mysterious, as the first Southport cricket club was not formed until 1859. It would seem that they must have been eleven men from the town who formed themselves into a team for this occasion. The second interesting point is the active involvement of the aristocracy, however minor. Many competition clubs have had such figureheads as president, as Edward Bootle-Wilbraham Lord Skelmersdale was for Ormskirk for many years. Few of these men, however, involved themselves in the club's welfare except as landlord and occasionally as a benefactor. Lord Skelmersdale appears to have been the only one who actually played himself.

This close involvement might suggest that the other members of the Ormskirk side were people with whom his Lordship might be expected to mix socially. What little additional evidence there is tends, however, to disaffirm this. Certainly his interest and patronage does not seem to have helped the Club to lead a settled existence in its first 50 years. Shortly after the 1853 game, it moved to a field on Southport Road, then in 1870 out to Aughton to a field at "Island House", Parrs Lane, only to return to Dyers Lane in Ormskirk two years later. Nor did his contacts among the upper and middle classes of Lancashire enable the Club to improve its fixture list. As late as 1878, the first year at their present ground in Brook

The first stages of preparing the Brook Lane Ground in Ormskirk 1877.

Lane, the opponents were largely from other rural areas such as Halsall, Croston, Pemberton and Newburgh.[25] It seems unlikely that the list was any more impressive in earlier days.

Possibly too great an emphasis has been placed on his Lordship as a player; for all we know the 7 runs recorded in 1853 may also be his career aggregate. Equally the assumption that he would choose to mix with his equals alone, is not necessarily valid. His interest in cricket did continue certainly. Two years before he succeeded to the title of Earl of Lathom in 1880, a match took place in Lathom Park between Lathom and Ormskirk, at which "a hearty vote of thanks was accorded to his lordship for his kindness and hospitality."[26] By now aged 43 he did not even play in his own team. It would probably be safer, therefore, to attribute his active involvement with Ormskirk in 1853 to youth, rather than to portray him as the leading light in a team of like minded and socially acceptable people.

The earliest surviving minute book records the affairs of the Club from 1869-90 and covers that period of the move to Aughton, the return to Dyers Lane and the final settlement at Brook Lane.

Despite the existence at this time of at least two other cricket clubs in Ormskirk, this is the period when Ormskirk C.C. became "the Club." By 1869 it was certainly not a village club, as one imagines a village side with its mix of squire, parson and a cross section of the rest of the community. There seems to have been a deliberate policy to make the Club more select socially and members became increasingly drawn from businessmen and the wealthier farmers.

This may well have been the result of the sons of the locally affluent, widening their horizons and contacts by education at boarding schools and the number of these increased rapidly in the second half of the 19th century. Of the influential members of this period the Ainscoughs were farmers and millers from Parbold, Lingard was a wealthy farmer, the Stretch's were local solicitors and the Blundells were stockbrokers.[27] Many of the others were concerned in cotton both in Ormskirk, where the proposed building of a cotton mill led to the Club losing its Dyers Lane ground, and of course in Liverpool. As with the towns along the Southport line, although to a lesser extent, the wealthy businessmen of Liverpool had moved to the pleasanter rural surroundings of Ormskirk commuting daily to their places of business.

By the late 1870s Ormskirk seems to have attracted the sort of people who were considered desirable, but not a fixture list which was likely to retain them for long. As much as anything else the three moves in that decade did not help, bearing in mind that the pitches could not have been of a very high standard, as each time plough land had to be levelled and made suitable for cricket. Until a permanent site could be found, there was little likelihood of the top clubs condescending to visit them. The Club must have felt that they had reached this desirable stage with the move from Aughton to Dyers Lane. In the words of Walter Stretch,

"A good pitch was laid, a new pavilion was built and a good deal of expense incurred in making a really good ground . . . In 1878 a company was formed in Ormskirk to build a cotton mill and unfortunately they fixed on the Cricket Field as the most suitable place for the mill and although the Club protested strongly at having their field taken from them, they had to give it up, without any compensation for all the money spent. This was the more annoying, as after hanging fire for a year or two the mill venture ended in smoke, but meantime the ground had been cut up and ruined."[28]

Mr. Stretch is in error as to the date. The matter first arose at the committee meeting of 20th July 1876, when the Secretary read out a notice to quit and it was "resolved to wait on Mr. Hale." Mr. Hale was Lord Derby's agent with whom they had dealt since moving there in 1873. By December of 1876 the Club obviously knew of the intention to build a cotton spinning mill and approached the company to ascertain the possibility of the Club still being able to play there in 1877.[29] But the company had already begun cutting the field up, and there is some uncertainty as to where they played that season. Certainly Mr. Hale attempted to charge them the £10 rent for that year, but the reply was that "under all the circumstances the Club considers it unfair that it should be called upon to pay."[30]

By this time an agreement had been made, in July 1877, to accept "Mr. Hale's offer of Bryers Lower Field, situate in Brook Lane", at a slightly higher rent of £12.[31] The tenancy agreement, however, was to commence on 2nd February 1878. There are several other resolutions in the minutes, which suggest that the Club wanted to move at an earlier date, if only to prepare the ground and to enable the members to have a practice area. It seems extremely doubtful that any matches were played there until the 1878 season, especially as in February of 1878 they were still arranging to have the new ground "in playable order."[32]

They certainly faced an uphill task with this new ground. The photograph on page 40 shows a threshing machine in the initial stages of cleaning the field of the corn which was about 5 ft. high. John Bryers, the previous tenant, had also left the fences in a very bad state of repair. The field, when cleared, was found to be 4 ft. higher in the middle than at the sides and had to be levelled. The pavilion, generally referred to as "the tent" was moved from its previous site and required repairs. All of this caused heavy expenditure, although the annual rent was offset by allowing a Mr. Snape to graze his cows in the field from April to October for £12. Understandably "during the playing of cricket or meetings of any kind, cows be not in the field."[33]

Again, as with Bootle, it seems strange that the Club did not seize this moment to secure its future by purchasing the land. Perhaps it was simply that the cost of such a venture was deemed prohibitive. It was not until 1922, that, in the face of rumoured building schemes in the neighbourhood, the Club raised through donations £500 towards the total cost of £750 to buy the Brook Lane site. It is worth noting that the chairman of the time, G.W. Blundell, was the prime mover and himself headed the subscription list with £250.[34]

Back in 1878 such a generous donation was not forthcoming and various fund raising efforts were conducted. A bazaar and soirees,[35] which those who have been to social events at Ormskirk in more recent times may find incongruous. Entertainments with the Christy Minstrels, one of which caused the abandonment of a committee meeting, as the secretary dolefully recorded, "the last member having left to hear the Christy Minstrels I closed the meeting."[36] Visits from the "Clown Cricketers of London", at which, in addition, there were stalls selling flowers, fruit and vegetables.[37] By dint of these efforts and the hard work of many members the Club managed to stay afloat, but they seem to have been regularly in debt in the first years at Brook Lane.

The Treasurer in 1884 detailed the state of affairs, which showed the Club to have overspent by £43-18-8. This seemed to justify raising the subscription from 10/6 to one guinea and asking Lord Derby to forgo the rent for the 1883 season.[38] However these draconian measures failed to stem the tide as the debt balance for 1884 was even greater at £48-16-0. The balance sheet for 1884 was made up of the following major items (in round figures).[39]

Receipts		Expenses	
Subscriptions	£ 60	Wages	£ 30
Gate money	£ 20	Rent	£ 12
Sheep grazing	£ 8	Cricket Goods	£ 25
Horse show	£ 3	Repairs	£ 15
Sports	£ 9	Sundry a/cs	£ 25
Christy Minstrels	£ 11		
	£111		£107

It perhaps helps to put into perspective the progress which the Club was making and its standing among other cricket clubs to compare this with the balance sheets of Liverpool in 1883 and Bootle in 1885.

Receipts	Liverpool[40]	Bootle[41]	Ormskirk
Subscriptions	1323	339	60
Gate money	138	15	20
Fund raising	nil	37	23
Sub-letting	nil	28	8
Expenses			
Wages	743	210	30
Rent	300	30	12
Cricket Goods	164	60	25
Repairs	—	16	15
Sundry a/cs	182	68	25

It is clear from this that, despite having been in existence for over 50 years, Ormskirk was still a very small cricket club. It is consequently surprising how quickly it came to the forefront of Merseyside clubs after these inauspicious beginnings. It could never hope to become a club on the scale of the Aigburth one; the nature of the town and the size of the population determined this.

The members in the 1880s knew how essential it was, not just to improve their playing facilities, but to change their predominantly parochial fixture list for one against opponents drawn from a much wider area. To this end, attempts were made, as early as 1883, to arrange fixtures with the three largest and most successful Merseyside clubs, Liverpool, Sefton and Birkenhead Park and also with Preston, Wigan and Warrington.[42] Apart from Warrington they all lost little time in turning down the offer and the secretary was instructed to issue "challenges" to the rather less august clubs of Southport Alexandra, Northern, Stanley and Wavertree.[43] Possibly as a result of this rebuff from the Merseyside clubs, Ormskirk appear to have looked eastwards for improved fixtures. In 1885 they joined the newly formed East Lancashire Cricket League. In the League's knockout cup they beat Middleton and Church before losing in the semi-finals to Darwen. There was apparently a huge crowd on the day of the match against Church at Brook Lane, over 700 paying at the gate.[44] Despite this success, the episode seems to have been only a passing flirtation with proper league cricket and the inclination still seemed to be to build up the Liverpool connection and the type of "friendly" cricket in vogue there.

The playing strength of the Club obviously did grow rapidly during the 1880s. Towards the end of the decade matches were played against Manchester, Bolton, Wigan, Preston, Chorley and Leyland as well as the majority of the top Merseyside clubs. Only the coveted fixture against Liverpool C.C. seems still to have eluded it, although it had clearly not given up trying. The minutes of February 1888 deferentially record that the secretary was

"requested to write to A.G. Steel Esq., and ask him if he could see his way to bring an eleven to Ormskirk some day during the coming season."[45]

By the 1890s Ormskirk was recognised as a worthwhile member of that loose federation of clubs known collectively as the Liverpool and District Clubs. Indeed by 1895 two of its players, the brothers T. and J. Ainscough, were deemed good enough to play for the representative Liverpool and District XI against Cambridge University.[46] Tom Ainscough was later to score 195 for them against Jessop's Gloucestershire side, the highest score ever made in these representative matches, on either side.[47]

Compared with Bootle C.C., Ormskirk's early development had been very slow. By 1891 when the present pavilion was first constructed, it was a rising star and most certainly this was due, to a great extent, to its finally becoming established at Brook Lane. Whilst it would always remain identifiably a closely knit small town club and different to all the other Competition clubs, in its competitiveness and its ability to attract and foster talent, it had put behind it for ever the village-like appearance of the first 50 years.

REFERENCES

1. H.S. Brown, The History of Bootle C.C. (Unpublished. 1942), p.1.
2. R. Brookes, *Never a Dull Moment : The Bootle Story* (Bootle Corporation 1968), p.19.
3. Ibid., p.19.
4. H.S. Brown, op. cit., p.2.
5. R. Brookes, op. cit., p.34.
6. R. Bowen, Cricket : *A History of its Growth and Development throughout the World* (Eyre & Spottiswood 1970), p.111.
7. Undated newspaper cutting in a scrapbook in the possession of Liverpool C.C.
8. Newspaper cutting — July 26th 1866 in a scrapbook op. cit.
9. Undated newspaper cutting in a scrapbook op. cit.
10. Undated newspaper cutting in a scrapbook op. cit. Clearly not a local newspaper as it refers to "Bootle, near Liverpool."
11. H.S. Brown, op. cit. p.4.
12. Ibid., p.8.
13. *Liverpool Daily Post* 5th July 1946.

14. H.S. Brown, op. cit. p.4.
15. Minutes of the Bazaar Committee, in the possession of Bootle C.C.
16. Undated newspaper cutting in a scrapbook op. cit.
17. Ibid.
18. Inside the front cover of a scorebook for 1881 in the possession of Bootle C.C.
19. *Porcupine* 13th December, 1864.
20. Undated newspaper eutting in a scrapbook in the possession of Bootle C.C.
21. Balance sheet dated October 31st 1883 — original document in the possession of Bootle C.C.
22. W. Stretch, *Ormskirk Cricket Club – a few particulars of its Progress and Records* (1935), p.4.
23. Interview with Ken Lea, secretary of Ormskirk C.C. 21st November, 1982.
24. Quoted in W. Stretch, op. cit., p.4.
25. Fixture card for 1878, original document in the possession of Ormskirk C.C.
26. Undated newspaper cutting in the possession of Ormskirk C.C.
27. Interview with K. Lea op. cit.
28. W. Stretch, op. cit. p.6.
29. Minute Book of Ormskirk C.C. in the possession of the Club 14th December 1876.
30. Ibid., February 1st 1878.
31. Ibid., July 11th 1877.
32. Ibid., February 1st 1878.
33. Ibid., March 6th 1878.
34. W. Stretch, op.cit., p.7.
35. Minute Book, op.cit., 21st December 1881.
36. Ibid., undated meeting between May 1871 and September 1873.
37. Ibid., 25th March 1878.
38. Ibid., 15th February 1883.
39. Ibid., 23rd January 1885.
40. Minute Book of Liverpool C.C., in the possession of Liverpool C.C. March 3rd 1884.
41. Balance Sheet for Bootle C.C. 1885, original document in the possession of the Bootle C.C.
42. Minute Book of Ormskirk C.C., op. cit., 26th September 1883.
43. Ibid., 28th November 1883.
44. W. Stretch, op. cit., p.9.
45. Minute Book, op. cit., February 27th 1888.
46. G.A. Brooking (ed), *The Complete History of Liverpool and District versus Colonial and Foreign Teams, First Class Counties and Cambridge University* (T.W. Gornall & Co. 1931), pp. 13-14.
47. Ibid., pp. 45-46.

CHAPTER THREE

Security of Tenure — The story of
The Birkdale Cricket Ground Company Limited

As can be seen from the early histories of many of the clubs, their greatest problem was in securing a permanent site. One of the ways of doing this which was used by three of the clubs, New Brighton, Liverpool and Southport, was to form a company to purchase the land. Thus the New Brighton District Cricket Company Ltd., 1882, the Liverpool and South West Lancashire Cricket Ground Co. Ltd., 1882 and the Birkdale Cricket Ground Co. Ltd., 1884 were all formed within the space of three years. Possibly the idea originated with one club and was copied by the other two but there is no evidence of this. There are however great similarities in the formation of the companies and their subsequent history and it is perhaps worthwhile to look at one of these more closely.

The Birkdale Club played its first match at Trafalgar Road on 25th May 1874 on part of a much larger plot of land which had only two months before been the subject of an agreement with the Weld-Blundell family and the Birkdale Park Land Company. The Articles of Agreement show that the Company purchased 250 acres at a cost of £20 per acre.[1] This particular land transaction was a later stage in the development of Birkdale which had begun when Thomas Weld-Blundell, the landowner first proposed the idea of Birkdale Park, as it was termed, in 1848. Despite the favourable terms at which the land, previously known as Aindow's Hills, was offered there does not seem to have been initially any great enthusiasm. Most of the land lay on the seaward side of the Liverpool to Southport Railway and consisted largely of waste and sandhills. The idea really took off as a result of the involvement of John Aughton an energetic and enterprising builder who came from Preston in 1850. Within ten years the area bounded by Westcliffe Road, Weld Road, York Road and Aughton Road was already well advanced with 124 occupied houses. By 1868 the number of streets had increased to eighteen as the development moved southwards towards the Cricket Club's future ground.[2]

The Land Company, when it leased the ground to the cricketers in 1874 had only granted a 9 year lease presumably so they could keep their options open. They already had plans to convert, at some future date a further 50 acres of Blundell's land into a "Park or Pleasure Gardens for the use of the respective lessees of the said land." The Birkdale Park was eventually laid out adjacent to Victoria Park with which it was combined in 1912 when the townships of Birkdale and Southport were amalgamated. The Company seem to have felt that the Cricket Club would ultimately be more suitably accommodated in the Park leaving the Trafalgar Road site free for more lucrative development.[3]

Certainly the Birkdale Cricket Club was not by 1883 in a very secure position, although they had, two years previously in June 1881, erected a pavilion which for its time was quite imposing at a cost of about £300. Similarly a contract had been made in February 1880 with two "Labourers" John Lloyd and Thomas Marshall of Birkdale, "to level, sod and lay with good turf sixty yards by forty yards of the Field" for which they were to be paid "one penny for every square yard thus completed."[4] The pavilion was to stand until 1965 by which time, although still structurally sound it had outlived its usefulness. When it was first built, however, it must have been an impressive building for cricketers more accustomed to changing in sheds and tents. The **Southport Visiter** of June 21st reported that

"the Birkdale Club which is leading a flourishing existence has made some improvements at its headquarters this season and the ground is now in capital condition. A very handsome and substantial pavilion has also been erected. The building is in the Queen Ann style with quaint windows, that over the centre doors having the initials of the Club worked out in stained glass. The interior comprises dressing rooms, a large and lofty main apartment fitted with a refreshment bar, beneath which is a capital cellar. A verandah runs in front of the pavilion and completes one of the best buildings of this kind we have ever seen."[5]

Both this and the ground improvement suggest that the Club fully expected their lease to be extended for a longer period. This confidence must have been somewhat dented by the letter they received in April 1883 from the Land Company's solicitor after they had applied for a renewal of the lease.

"We brought your application for an undertaking to renew your present lease of the cricket ground for a further term of 7 years before the Directors at their meeting yesterday and they instructed us to state that they will be glad to do what they can in the future to assist the Club but that there are changes in prospect which prevent them giving a definite reply to your proposal for the present.

It is in contemplation to form a Park at Birkdale but nothing definite has yet been decided; perhaps it might be arranged in the future for your Club to have the use of some of the land in the Park."[6]

The proposal referred to was presumably one which either dealt with the question of a longer lease or some other more permanent arrangement.

That the cricketers had already thought of forming a company can be seen in some correspondence in 1882 between the Club Treasurer and Solicitor, R.S. Potts, and an accountant and mortgage broker J.H. Plummer. In a letter of February 14th Plummer states, "trusting there will be no slip you might look up the Articles so that we may get the Company registered at an early date."[7] His fears of a "slip" seem to have been justified albeit temporarily, for there was no further mention of the company for almost another two years.

What seems certain to have been the catalyst was the letter from the Land Company with its broad hint that the Club's days at Trafalgar Road were limited. The company was formed in January 1884 and in the same month an agreement was made to purchase the land at, as the prospectus later described, "a very favourable rate." The Land Company's philanthropic gesture must also be weighed against the fact that they received £550 for the 4 1/2 acre site which seems at face value to have cost them only £90 ten years earlier.[8] The site is shown on the scaled down plan on page 50.[9]

The prospectus, of which 200 copies were optimistically printed, was sent out in June to Club members largely and a few other local people who the directors felt would be interested in such a venture. The objective, clearly stated in bold type, was to afford "the members of the Birkdale Cricket Club an opportunity of retaining in their possession the present cricket ground." The directors pointed out the unlikelihood of "any immediate prospect of a large pecuniary advantage," yet, almost as an afterthought added that should the ground ever no longer be required for the purpose of cricket and other games that "the shareholders will remain possessed of a valuable property."[10]

The response to this opportunity was initially disappointing. Of the 1000 shares offered, at £1 a share, less than half (492) were taken up. Henry Crowley, described as 'Gentleman', who lived opposite the ground in Trafalgar Road, took 100 shares, as did W.H. Stead, similarly a 'Gentleman' living in Trafalgar Road and W.E. Smith, a solicitor. These last two were both directors of the Company as was G.C. Chamberlain, a stockbroker who had 20 shares, Herbert Horton, a chemical manufacturer (20) and Thomas Hatch a shipbroker who purchased 30.[11]

49

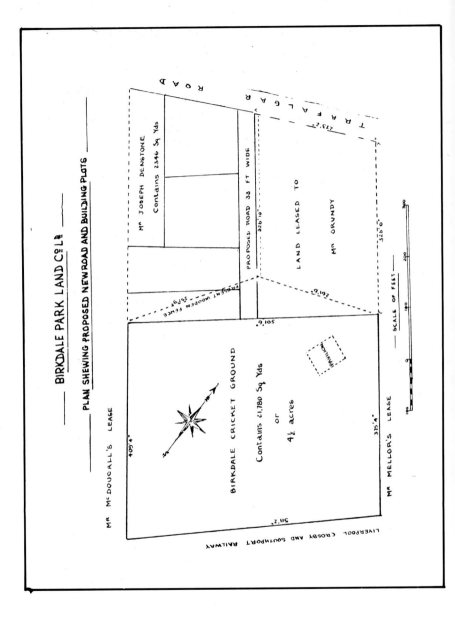

The site at Trafalgar Road at the time of its purchase, 1884.

50

From the addresses and occupations of the 17 original shareholders, their wealth is indisputable, yet the majority were indisposed to make more than a gesture of support. When compared with the cost of the shares in the Liverpool company of £25 and the alacrity with which they were taken up, the response at Birkdale seems niggardly. So poor was it that when the costs of forming the Company were totalled, it was found necessary to obtain a private mortgage of £450 from a Mary Eccles. The books for this first year were finally balanced by a £30 rent from the Cricket Club and a loan of £70 from W.H. Stead.

The Company had promised little "pecuniary advantage" and seems over the years to have been able to keep to this. Annual dividends were declared from 1890 to the outbreak of the First World War and varied between 2% and $3\frac{1}{2}\%$. Even this small amount is surprising since the Company's income was almost solely dependent on the amount they charged the Cricket Club for rent. Pre 1939 this was never more than £40 per annum and indeed, during the 1914-18 War, it was as low as £20, as a result of a reduced membership of the Club and its use of the ground being considerably curtailed.[12]

Despite its financial lack of success, it has achieved the objective of ensuring the continued presence of the Club. The shares have changed hands many times over the years, more often than not as a result of a shareholder's decease. One shareholder, however, may have considered himself unfortunate in the way he lost his holdings.

Louis Seidel, a German who had come to Southport some time before the First World War, was a Professor of Music taking in students at his home in Bridge Street. Whether he had any interest in cricket or not is unknown; there is certainly no record of his having played. Nevertheless the Company books record that in 1912 he purchased 31 shares, not in itself particularly significant. Whether he remained in England during the war is also unknown, but by 1923 he was living in Saxony. That year the Company received, as presumably all other companies did, a circular which stated, among other things, that

> "pursuant to the terms of the Treaty of Versailles, all Property
> Rights and Interests within His Majesty's Dominions or
> Protectorates, belonging to German Nationals"

should be transferred to the Public Trustee Office. Seidel's shares were duly handed over and in February 1926 were bought by a Club member from the Public Trustee Office. It is probable that the Professor received no recompense.[13]

Whilst the shares were held by quite a number of people with their ownership changing hands normally as a result of a death, the

Company other than charging an annual rent does not seem to have involved itself in its tenant's affairs. From the time of the Great War, however, one man seems to have made a determined effort to gain a controlling majority of these shares.

James Mulgrew, a wealthy provision merchant, had with his brother first played for Birkdale in 1888. He was at different times, and often at the same time secretary, treasurer, chairman and captain. At times he seems to have run the Club almost single-handedly. In retrospect it is possible to interpret this involvement in different ways. In a eulogy written shortly after his death in 1953, he is described in the following way

> "Such was the unshakeable faith of James Mulgrew that the Club must survive whatever the hazards, that he never shrank from the task of meeting all financial commitments from his own resources, which became more or less an all the year round loan. The Club owe him a very deep debt of gratitude for steering them through very dark days when their very survival looked to be in the balance."[14]

Since then others, who knew him, have suggested that the "dark days" were to some extent a result of the way in which the Club was run and the constraints which were imposed on it by him in terms of possible improvement and expansion which might have led it out of the depression. Throughout his long involvement with the Club and especially from 1919-50 as Treasurer, he held the purse strings. His power, however, was far greater than that given him by his offices, for not only was the Club continually in debt to him, but he had also taken up the Birkdale Cricket Ground Company's mortgage of £450. Additionally and perhaps more crucially he had over a period of years, purchased sufficient shares to gain control of the Company.

> 1910 —   65 shares
> by 1920 — 115 shares
> by 1941 — 215 shares
> by 1951 — 319 shares out of 558 issued.[15]

Up to 1939 these shares were bought at face value, but thereafter, they cost him as little as 5/- a share. It could, of course, be argued that he collected these to safeguard the Club, but equally it could be seen as a deliberate move to ensure that the affairs of the Company, as of the Club, could be rigidly controlled by him.

Southport & Birkdale C.C. 1924
From left to right (top): *J. Mulgrew, W.A. Warren, W. Howard, D. Sutton,*
J.R. Harvey Blackhurst, J.A. Dean, C. Wood, S.E. Rigg, W.E. Beckett,
S.G. Whitehead, N. Howard and R.E. Thorne.

What is indisputable is that the subsequent, although relative, affluence of the Club dates from the middle 1950s with such ventures as a new pavilion, annual county matches, squash courts, snooker tables and an all the year round social club.

His brother inherited his shares but not his consuming interest in Southport and Birkdale cricket, nor his desire to control and was only too willing to allow his shares to be bought by the three trustees which the Company appointed. They were, over a period of time, able to obtain all the remaining shares, despite the fact that a few of the shareholders could not be traced. This problem was solved by the simple expedient of placing an advertisement in the local paper of the area in which these shareholders were last known to have resided, giving notice that if the Company was not informed, within a month, to the contrary their shares would be taken up by the trustees.[16] In this way the Cricket Club was finally freed of any possibility of its ground being used or abused for any other purpose than that laid down in the 1884 prospectus.

REFERENCES

1. Copy Agreement for Leases of Lands at Birkdale, original document in the possession of Southport and Birkdale Cricket Club, p.1.
2. F.A. Bailey, *A History of Southport* (Angus Downie 1955),
3. Copy Agreement for Leases of Lands at Birkdale, op. cit., p.5.
4. Contract, dated the 9th February 1880, original document held by the Southport and Birkdale Cricket Club.
5. *Southport Visiter,* 21st June 1881.
6. Copy letter, dated Liverpool 10th April 1883 from Oliver Jones Billson & Co., original document in the possession of Southport and Birkdale Cricket Club.
7. Letter, dated 14th February 1882, original document in the possession of Southport and Birkdale Cricket Club.
8. From the documents which have survived a solicitor friend feels that it is not possible to say precisely what profit the Land Company made on this agreement, but it was clearly a handsome one. The Cricket Ground Company also had to pay £300 to the Weld-Blundell family for its co-operation, presumably in the granting of the 999 year lease.
9. At the bottom of the plan Mr. Potts has written "This is the Plan referred in the Agreement between the Birkdale Land Co. Ltd., and Mr. R.S. Potts. Dated 31st December, 1883."
10. From the *Birkdale Cricket Ground Company Limited Prospectus* several copies of which are still in the possession of Southport and Birkdale Cricket Club.
11. From the Cricket Ground Company's Allotment Book, in the possession of Southport and Birkdale Cricket Club.
12. Minute Book of the Birkdale Cricket Ground Co. Ltd., in the possession of Southport and Birkdale Cricket Club.

14. K.H. Porter, Twelve Decades of Cricket 1859-1979; Being the Story of Southport and Birkdale Cricket Club. This lengthy work was written over a long period of time by Mr. Porter who was the Honorary Secretary 1931-32, 1940-41 and 1947-82. The section quoted was written about 1956. Sadly it has never been published except in a very abridged form in a centenary brochure of the Club in 1974. A copy of the full work is in the possession of Southport and Birkdale Cricket Club.
15. Minute Book, op. cit.
16. Copies of advertisements in several local newspapers are in the possession of Southport and Birkdale Cricket Club. These include the Kent and Sussex Courier, the North Staffs Times and Echo and three Wirral newspapers. The wording is the same in each apart from the names. The following example is from the Kent and Sussex Courier of February 1954

"Birkdale Cricket Ground Co. Ltd.

Take notice that the following member of the Birkdale Cricket Ground Co. Ltd., who has failed during a period of 6 years or more to attend in person or by proxy at any General Meeting of the Company is liable to have his share or shares in the Company sold in accordance with the Company's Articles unless within the period of one month required by such Articles he delivers to the Company at its registered office a notice in writing stating the address of his present residence or some person produces to the Company at its registered office evidence of being entitled to such share or shares

John Sidney Crowley"

CHAPTER FOUR

The World's First Industrial Recreation Club

Lancashire provided both the starting point and the impetus for the Industrial Revolution and by the 1840s much of the wealth of Britain was generated through the factories of the county. Of the towns which are today represented in the Liverpool Competition only one, St. Helens Recreation C.C., grew up amid this manufacturing explosion. Most of the others were on the fringe of this activity and even Liverpool was a commercial rather than an industrial centre.

St. Helens in 1847, the year in which the Club was formed, was suffering like most of the industrial north from the twin problems of overpopulation and pollution. There had been a doubling of the population in the years 1830-45, and the provisions for sewage and water which had been reasonable for a town of 6,000 people were by 1847 hopelessly inadequate. The sewage drained into a central brook running through the town, and a resident described it as "on open ditch running among the dwellings for at least a mile and exposing in its course an evaporating surface of filth but a few yards less than an acre in extent."[1] Of the water supply, the **St. Helens Intelligencer** commented on the "frequent complaints of the filthy, noxious unhealthy condition" of it.[2] Possibly even more unpleasant especially for the unaccustomed visitor, was the smell which was the town's most outstanding characteristic and which was apparently caused by the action of hydrochloric acid on calcium sulphide from the alkali works.

It is only fair to add that, except for its peculiar smell, the conditions were no different from those prevailing in most other industrial towns and that it was not by 19th century standards particularly unhealthy. The mortality figures were well below that of Liverpool, Leeds or Manchester and even in the cholera outbreaks such as that of 1849, a relatively small number of victims, about 100, were recorded.

In the 1840s the predominant industry in the St. Helens area was still coal-mining, but this was the decade in which the emphasis began to shift and the glass and chemical industries expanded. Out of one of these new industries emerged an idea, which seems totally incongruous for an area and an age in which the guiding principle was largely one of the exploitation of the work force in the pursuit of profit.

In 1847 Pilkingtons the St. Helens glassmaking firm formed a Works Recreation Club for the benefit of its employees. This was certainly the first recreation club in the country and, bearing in mind Britain's position as the first industrial nation, probably the first in the world.[3] The date 1847 is when the outdoor facilities for recreation were first provided. It is unlikely that the directors of the firm suddenly conceived the idea of such a recreation club and more likely that it evolved from previous activities which the company had sponsored and encouraged. Its very beginnings, probably, lay in the evangelical spirit of the non-conformist Pilkington family and their holding of bible reading sessions. They later built a reading room on the firm's premises, from which employees could borrow books. That developed into a kind of leisure centre where indoor games such as chess, dominoes, billiards and bagatelle were played. From this and the practice of organising works outings and dances may have come the demand for outside games with cricket as the first and most important activity.[4]

It would be a mistake, however, to exaggerate the benevolence of the Pilkingtons. It is true that they were pioneers in the field of industrial recreational provision, as it is true that they looked after their employees in other ways such as engaging a schoolmaster to teach the three R's to the boys and young men in their employment, albeit in their own time. Despite the Factory Act of 1833 which laid down that children under 13 should have two hours of such schooling in the firm's time, there was no obligation for Pilkingtons to comply. This and all the later factory reforms up to 1867 did not apply to glassmaking, being primarily aimed at the abuses in the textile mills.

Some of the highly skilled glassworkers were paid very good wages, but Pilkingtons like most employers never paid more than they needed to. Even in the slack years like 1849, of the 404 employees in the works 152 received more than 30/- a week, and a few key workers such as the sheet glassblowers more than 50/-. The majority of the labour force (254), which included women and young boys, earned less than 10/- a week. It is always difficult to compare these wages with those of other trades. From lists of wages it is often impossible to discover the age of the employee, the exact nature of the work and the hours, without which the wage list becomes far less meaningful. Barker suggests that, among the skilled trades, ironfounders earned up to £2 per week and skilled engineers a little more, but that for the general run of skilled craftsmen, builders, masons and carpenters the weekly wage would have been around 30/-.[5] This is similar to the wage index produced by Phelps, Brown and Hopkins of a daily rate of 4/1d for building craftsmen in Southern England 1847-52.[6] But for the unskilled adult male worker generally the average was 10s-12s for this period, which was not unlike that of the unskilled employee at Pilkingtons.

Where the glassworkers were certainly in a better position than most other craftsmen was in the relatively short working week of around 40 hours. Again, however, this stems more from the practicalities of the industry than from considerate management.

"A complete charging, melting and cooling cycle usually took about twenty four hours. The working itself took rather less than half that time, usually about ten hours. This meant that even at the maximum rate of production the glassmakers were bound to have about twenty four hours off at the end of each ten hour shift. They started at 6.00 a.m. on Monday morning and worked until Monday afternoon, began the second shift about 4.00 p.m. on Tuesday, the third at 2.00 a.m. on Thursday and the fourth about noon on Friday, finishing work for the week late of Friday night. This left them with Saturday and Sunday completely free."[17]

The unskilled and semi-skilled workers involved in the preparation and cleaning up process would, of course, work considerably longer hours, although they too would be off work for much of the weekend.

Pilkingtons seem to have been considered good employers, and certainly there was a tradition among the non-confirmist employers of the 19th century of looking after their work-force. But we need to look behind this image of benevolent paternalism for their motives in providing recreation facilities.

The most important factor lies in the nature of the industry itself. It was a highly specialised one in which there was a scarcity of labour. The key workers were the glassblowers and in the 1840s there were probably less than 200 in Britain and even more significantly less than 50 sheet glassblowers. In 1845 the duty on window glass, which had been levied since the 1690s was repealed and the demand for the services of these sheet glassblowers increased enormously. The possession of such men could make or break a firm, even one as established as Pilkingtons, who had forseen the implications of repeal and had taken the precaution of binding their glassblowers with new seven year contracts shortly before it. Even so, as Barker explains the demand for sheet glass was beyond the abilities of the existing men to supply.

"Local recruitment was a satisfactory method of obtaining a gradual supply of skilled labour over a period of time by way of seven year apprenticeships, but it was quite useless as a means of meeting a sudden emergency, such as arose in 1845."[8]

Pilkingtons were forced to look further afield and brought in workers from France and Belgium who, of course, could and did demand high rates of pay. The resentment which this created among the local workers and their realisation of their true worth prompted a few to break their contracts and offer themselves to rival glassmakers. Ultimately Pilkingtons were able, through law, to recover these few adventurers, but realising that their contracts would eventually expire, it became imperative for the firm to find ways of securing, on a long term basis, the loyalty of their key employees. In this preoccupation lay the germ of the idea of providing recreational facilities.

Cricket was the first and most important activity at the Recreation Club and this is not altogether surprising. The game was already popular in the neighbourhood. St. Helens C.C. had been in existence for four years and used a ground behind the Raven Inn until 1858 when the land was required for the new railway station.[9] It is strange how often the railways, which in many ways were beneficial to cricket clubs, also forced them to move their grounds. There were also a number of church sides, so there existed, at the very outset, teams for the Recreation Club to play against.[10]

Of equal importance was the interest, of some members of the Pilkington family, in the game. William Roby Pilkington, the eldest grandson of the founder, was an enthusiastic player. Aged 20 in 1847, it seems likely that he would have been one of the leading lights in the Cricket Club and certainly its most influential player. Both he and his brother Thomas played for a St. Helens team against the All England XI in May 1853,[11] and one would assume that they were competent players, although there is always the possibility of their exercising droit du seigneur.

At first sight, the hours which the employees worked, with their free weekends, suggests that this would have been a contributing factor in their choosing to play cricket, a game which consumes large periods of time. It was, indeed unusual for workers to have even a half day on Saturday, let alone the whole day. Additionally the cost to the worker of these recreational facilities was small. The workforce contributed 1d a week towards the cost of maintaining the Club and in later years paid a small subscription to whichever section of the Club they wished to belong.[12] Whether they had to pay such a subscription in 1847 is not known, as the minutes of the Recreation Club only go back to 1863, but it would only have been a relatively small payment. Both this low playing cost and greater leisure time suggests that there would have been a wider social mix in the cricket teams than we have seen in the other clubs. However, I am not so sure. Some of the directors of the Company played or were otherwise closely involved in cricket right through the 19th century. In 1893, for example, the team was captained by Ernest Pilkington the great grandson of the founder.[13] It seems questionable that their good relationships with the workforce would have extended to spending their leisure hours together. Even as late as the 1930s, there was a definite feeling on the shop floor, that the cricket team was for the white collar workers, although this has largely disappeared.[14] On the other hand one cannot ignore the possibility that the Pilkingtons captained sides of men from among the general workforce in much the same way as the great landowners of the 18th and early 19th century ran their village or estate sides. There is however no evidence of workers at Pilkingtons being taken on for their cricketing abilities.

I am inclined to the view that the general workforce did use the facilities for playing cricket, not as players for the St. Helens Recreation Club team, but rather in games played amongst themselves either on a casual ad hoc basis or in more organised matches between different departments of the firm. Today this is certainly the way cricket and soccer are enjoyed by most of the members of the Recreation Club. Indeed in many ways, the inter-departmental games are the main feature of the cricket programme.

St. Helens Recreation Club is and always has been different from the other 15 Clubs. It is the most recent member of the Competition, joining as late as 1953, when Preston were more or less obliged to leave. Pressure had been exerted on Preston in the 1940's by the Corporation who owned their ground, for the Club to play league cricket. In answer the Club had produced copies of the **Liverpool Daily Post** which printed a weekly "league" table and its departure had been postponed temporarily. The pressure was renewed in the early 1950s, probably when the Preston Corporation realised what everyone else knew, that the Competition was no more than a newspaper league. Preston C.C. joined the Northern League which, geographically at least, was the most appropriate place for it to be.[15]

The Preston Club had grown up on similar lines to the other competition clubs. Both its attitude to the game and its largely middle class membership were in the traditional mould, which we have seen at Aigburth, Bootle and Southport. Initially St. Helens was not as good a team as Preston nor were its players as socially acceptable and there was a certain amount of, largely unspoken, antipathy towards them. By the 1950s, however, social divisions were much less rigidly defined and adhered to and the arrivistes presented much less of a culture shock than they would have done in earlier days. Certainly in the 19th century it would have been inconceivable for a works team to have been invited to join the Competition. In 1953 St. Helens was not, by any means, the only club wishing to affiliate itself, and that it was accepted ahead of more traditional clubs, tends to support the view that many of the team and those who ran the Club were not from the shop floor.

Nevertheless the fact that they have always been a works team and subsidised places them apart from the others. The degree of subsidy is hard to assess. If anything, it has increased over the years, largely because, whilst the maintenance costs have risen, the size of the workforce and thus its total weekly contribution has fallen dramatically. Today each employee contributes 25p a week but this is not compulsory and a small part of it goes towards a monthly draw. What remains after the prize money is given out, goes to the Recreation Club. Assuming that they all contributed, in 1984, the 6,000 or so employees could not have given more than about £56,000 to Recreation, whereas the maintenance costs alone were nearly £1/4 million. Moreover this figure does not include such hidden subsidies as wages, which all the other clubs have to fund through subscriptions, bar takings or other money raising activities. Not surprisingly this has become a target for the cost conscious accountants of the firm, who argue that the participants in the various sections of the Recreation Club should pay a more realistic subscription. The St. Helens player who is an employee pays £8 a year to the cricket section, and even those who are not employees but choose to play there, only pay £25.[16] It seems doubtful that the cricketers will be able to resist this pressure for long, since the accountants will doubtless be fully aware that, on average at the other clubs, players are unlikely to pay less than £35, and in many cases considerably more.

REFERENCES

1. T.C. Barker and J.R. Harris, *A Merseyside Town in the Industrial Revolution : St. Helens 1750-1900* (Cass, 1954), p.39.
2. *St. Helens Intelligencer,*5th June 1850.
3. H. Logan, *Early Days of the Recs Club* (Cullet no. 2 Pilkington's Magazine 1929), p.25.
4. Ibid., p.25.
5. T.C. Barker, *Pilkington Brothers and the Glass Industry* (George Allen and Unwin Ltd. 1972), pp. 106-107.
6. E.A. Wrigley and R.S. Schofield, *The Population History of England 1541-1871* (Arnold 1981), Appendix 9, p.640.
7. T.C. Barker op. cit., pp. 108-109.
8. Ibid., p.102.
9. H. Logan, op. cit., p.25.
10. Interview with Mrs. Stubbs (Archivist at Pilkingtons), 24th January 1983.
11. *Wigan Times,* 13th May, 1853.
12. Interview with Mrs. Stubbs, op. cit.

13. Minute Book of the Cricket Section of the Recreation Club, 1893.
14. Interview with E. Tatlock (ex Chairman of the Cricket Section), 24th January 1983.
15. Interview with H. Wolfe, (retired sports editor of the Liverpool Echo), 10th November 1982.
16. Interviews with E. Tatlock and Mrs. Stubbs, op. cit.

CHAPTER FIVE
The changing fortunes of a Cricket Club —
Huyton C.C.

For the Competition cricketer today the annual visit to Huyton is seldom the most eagerly anticipated event. Its setting, its ground and its facilities fall way below those of the other clubs and, although this cannot be true, in ones memory the games at Huyton always seem to have been played in a persistent light drizzle. The Club seems to have stood on the verge of extinction for so long, being saved time after time by the loyalty and hard work of a few committed players and officials. At no other Competition Club has the nature of its surroundings changed so drastically. It exists today, almost as if in a vacuum, playing a game which is an irrelevance to the inhabitants of the houses and high rise flats which overlook it. At best the Club and its activities are ignored, at worst it becomes a target for the mindless vandalism of the bored and alienated youth of the area.

Yet largely because of this lack of support and finance, the self-help way in which the Club is run may be closer to how all the Competition clubs were in their early stages. The members cut the grass, prepare the wickets, run the bar and perform numerous maintenance jobs themselves. In this close involvement perhaps lies the intense loyalty which has enabled the Club to survive, when it would have been much easier for the members to call it a day and move on to Sefton or Ormskirk or St. Helens where the greatest demand on them would be to pay their subscriptions.

The Huyton C.C. has held the ground behind St. Michael's Church for an unbroken period of 126 years and it is possible that a Huyton cricket team played there even before 1860. Although no primary evidence for this can be found, several later newspaper articles talk about the villagers of Huyton having a Club which failed in the late 1850s. The Centenary Souvenir Programme published by the Club in 1960 says,

> "it is believed that there was a cricket club in Huyton before 1860. It was a kind of villagers club and a ground was obtained at a peppercorn rent from the Earl of Derby."[1]

The 1850 6 inch ordnance survey map, however, has no reference to a cricket ground, although there is a field similar in shape to the present ground and on the same site. From 1860 we know a great deal about the Cricket Club, because the original minutes have survived. These make no reference to a villagers club and the fact that expenses in the first year included the cost of laying the square and of acquiring equipment to start playing suggests that any earlier club had been a rather primitive one.

"At a meeting held in Huyton, the 7th May 1860 for the purpose of forming a Cricket Club, the following gentlemen were present: Mr. H.R. Whistler, Mr. Alex Eccles, Mr. Wm. Evans, Mr. Tho. Evans, Mr. Geo. Byrd, Mr. J. Priestley Tate and Mr. E. Moult."[2]

Even up to quite recent times Huyton C.C. was known as "the Villagers", a nickname which conjures up images of the traditional village cricket club, but this it quite clearly never was.[3] The involvement of the residents of Huyton village was small. From a census of 1850, none of the 45 householders named appear in the list of the 28 members of the Club in 1860.[4] It is debatable even whether by 1860 Huyton was a village in the true sense of the word. The population of Huyton doubled in the years 1801-1861 from 2013 to 4054, which was not, in comparison with many other Lancashire towns, all that drastic an increase. Considering that Huyton lay close to the very first passenger railway which connected Liverpool and Manchester, one might well have expected its population increase to have been even greater. In fact the impact of the railway seems, in purely numerical terms to have been surprisingly slight, with the increase slowing down after 1830 rather than accelerating. The real influence of the railway can be seen more closely in the maps on page 66. The urbanisation of Huyton left its original nucleus largely untouched, but the geographical centre moved away from the Church and cricket ground on the junction of Derby Road and Huyton Lane to the railway station. But it was the type, rather than the amount of development, which was important. It was not industrial urbanisation but suburbia of the kind more common to Southport and the other towns along the Southport to Liverpool line. Despite its situation in the centre of the Lancashire industrial and commercial heartland, Huyton was never an industrial town. There were, it is true, a number of collieries to the east, but the nearest to the "village" centre was at Huyton Quarry about a mile away. Most of the newcomers which the railway brought were not colliers, but the professional and merchant middle classes. They settled in large residences south of the railway line in Huyton Park and along Roby Road, and it was these people rather than the established families of the area who were instrumental in setting up the Cricket Club. The first committee chairman Alexander Eccles, who seems typical of this new breed, was a cotton broker living in Huyton Park. Among other members living there were Andrew Walker, a brewer and the Gardiners, James and William who were sons of a timber merchant.[5] Exactly when they settled in Huyton Park is not known, but they could not have been there long, as this residential area was not developed until the 1850s.

One can safely assume that the seven gentlemen, who met "for the purpose of forming a Cricket Club", were friends and also that the other 21 who joined them in that first year, were similarly acquainted with one or more of the original seven. This meeting took place on the 7th May and in less than three weeks, the first match was played at Huyton against the Bootle C.C. It would have been impossible, in such a short time, to prepare for cricket a piece of arable or even pasture land and this tends to confirm the existence of a cricket field on this site before 1860. That they were able to attract such a well established side like Bootle for their first fixture shows that at least some of the first committee were very well connected. The match resulted in a draw, the only notable feature being the large number of extras, 31 including 17 wides out of a total of 102 in Huyton's innings.[6] Despite this, the fact that Huyton were not thrashed points to Mr. Eccles, in 1860 aged 36, and his friends not being novices at the game.

Other matches that year were played against Princes Park, Parkside and Aigburth on a home and away basis and a return match against Bootle. One rather surprising fact from the 1860 score sheets, is that only four of the seven founding members actually played in these fixtures and only one, the Honorary Treasurer, J. Priestley Tate played regularly. This does make their motive in forming the Club rather more complex. It could not have been simply a case of wishing to provide for themselves a venue for playing cricket. Assuming that their motive was not a purely altruistic one, why did seven apparently well-to-do gentlemen go to the not inconsiderable expense and trouble of forming a cricket club for which only one of them intended to play regularly? Since the only records are the minutes which tell us what they did but seldom why, any answer to this question must be speculative.

Probably it had more to do with the status of their 'new' town. Similar residential areas of Liverpool and Manchester, cities with which these men, through their occupations, would have been familiar, had their select cricket clubs. If Huyton was to be considered socially on a comparable plane to these, then it too should have its cricket club. The Club would become not only the place for cricket to be played, but a means of socialising with those whom they wished to meet. For it to attract what was considered a suitable type of person, the club should be no makeshift affair. Their success in achieving this objective can be gauged by the speed with which it became fully established both in cricketing terms and as a club.

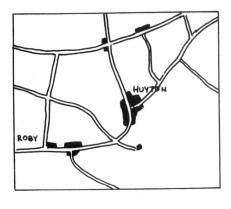

1. Based on
   Sherriff's *1828* Map.

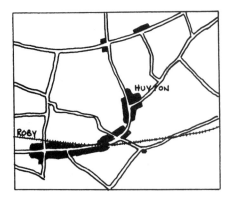

2. Based on *1850*
   Ordnance Survey Map.

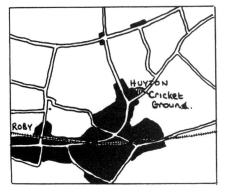

3. Based on *1892*
   Ordnance Survey Map.

The urban development of Huyton.

There are many indications of their intentions recorded in the minutes, not least the decision at the very first meeting that Mr. Eccles be "requested to draw up a code of rules to be observed by the 'Huyton C.C.' based on the rules enforced by the 'Liverpool C. Club'."[7] Although basing their rules on the best club in the district did not automatically give them equivalent status, it is still remarkable how quickly they organised a fairly full fixture list. From only eight games in 1860, Huyton played 18 two years later and many of the better sides on Merseyside were among its opponents which included Bootle, New Brighton, Anfield, Aigburgh, St. Helens (Town), Birketts XI (Liverpool 2nd team), Fairfield and Dingle as well as Manchester. The majority of these fixtures were on a Saturday afternoon, but it is significant that five were held mid-week, two of these being two-day games, clearly occasions in which only the leisured or professional classes could participate.[8]

Certainly there was no shortage of money among these early members. There was a 10/- entrance fee to the Club plus £1 (later £1-1-) annual subscription, but even more indicative of wealth was the manner in which the Treasurer was given carte blanche by the members agreeing to make up any deficit at the end of each season. In 1861, for example, each of them had to pay an additional 15/-.[9] Whenever any large item of expenditure arose, there were a large number of individuals prepared to make donations to cover it. In 1863 it was decided to lay a bowling green and build a pavilion. Of the 64 members in that year nearly a quarter of them gave donations of either £5 or £10 towards the cost.[10] And again in 1866, when the pavilion was improved, £105 was raised in the same way.[11] The pavilion had cost only £60 originally and must have been a fairly basic structure, although an additional £42 was spent on fittings and decoration. It had, in any case, a very short life being replaced in 1875 by the present pavilion.

The healthy financial state which the Club enjoyed in those early days can be seen in the profit of £71 for 1864, despite the relatively large capital investment of the previous season.

The membership grew rapidly throughout the early 1860s reaching a peak in 1866 when 93 paid the full subscription and another 31 'non-resident' members paid 10/6d. Members such as Lord Derby, Lord Sefton, Sir Thomas Birch and two Members of Parliament, C. Turner and A.H. Egerton attest to the esteem which the Club enjoyed. By then a professional/groundsman was employed and in 1870, only ten years after its formation, the Club could afford to engage both a professional, J. Unsworth, for 27 weeks at 30/- a week and a groundsman at 14/-. Although there is no balance sheet for this year, the expenses were approximately as follows:

Wages	£70
Rent	£12
Rates plus Taxes	£ 4
Maintenance	£12
(This seems a very low figure and suggests that materials may have been donated)	
Transport	£ 2

The total of £100 was easily covered by the subscriptions which were, at least, £128.[12]

In comparison with some of the other clubs, which in their early days were very insecure, Huyton went from strength to strength very rapidly. This was largely a consequence of the founders having obtained a ground on which no enormous initial expenditure was necessary, their determination, hard work and affluence and the relatively small annual expenses. It had very rapidly become what Alexander Eccles and his friends had intended, a successful and respected gentlemen's club and for almost a century it remained so.

It would be tedious to chart in detail the progress since that first decade, but some idea may be gained from highlighting three distinct periods, the Great War, the 1930s and the 1960s.

Little cricket was played during the 1914-18 war, mainly because so many of the cricketers enlisted, 56 members are included on the Club's Roll of Honour. The committee continued to meet as both bowls and tennis were still played regularly, and the minutes of the meetings for 1915-19 are very revealing of the patriotic, middle class attitudes towards the 'Great Game', and of the pressures to which the young men were subjected. In 1915 the secretary mentions that

"he had received complaints about the Club employing 2 men of military age. The recruiting sergeants had visited the 2 men in question and urged them to join. It was decided that Mr. H. Eccles should quietly tell the men it was their duty to join, but that no pressure should be put upon them."[13]

The men Barrell and Davies did in fact enlist later that year and it is pleasant to record that they both survived and enjoyed many successful years as professionals in the Competition.

At the Annual General Meetings throughout this period, the President, there being no cricket on which to comment, summarised the situation in the War. In 1917 "he hoped that now she (England) was ready to give all our Enemies what they had asked for and what they deserved."[14] The following year

"he alluded to the unfortunate position of the Allies, but that they had a valuable asset in America, who he hoped and was sure, would follow out their principles and that with their full help we should succeed in beating our Enemies."[15]

Finally in 1919

"he referred to the conclusion of hostilities and though we had not actually signed the Peace Treaty he hoped that we were out of the wood and though we had no doubt troubles at home he was confident our Prime Minister Mr. Lloyd George would see us through."[16]

The Club survived the War years largely because the President, Harry Eccles son of Alexander had guaranteed to pay off any deficit which was incurred. Consequently there was no delay in cricket being resumed and the immediate post-war years of 1920-23 were by far the most successful ones the Club ever enjoyed.[17] Although it never again enjoyed comparable success, the members continued for another 40 years to lead a very comfortable existence, and this seems to have been due, in no small measure, to the emergence of one very influential figure, Tom Stone.

He had been educated at Marlborough, a school popular among the middle classes of Merseyside, possibly because of its "reputation for scholarship in those philistine times. It represented the better class of school."[18] The numerous accounts of life there by such people as Siegfried Sassoon and John Betjeman detail both the bestiality of the place and the ways in which one could survive it.[19] The school's motto was 'Virtute, Studio, Ludo' with the emphasis decidedly on the 'Ludo', and one can well imagine that Tom Stone and other Merseyside boys with games ability like the Steel brothers of Liverpool C.C., would have enjoyed the privileges and esteem which the system gave them. It is scarcely surprising that his life at Marlborough and subsequent success at Oxford, where he boxed, played rugby and golf as well as cricket, should have moulded him into a dominant personality. He captained the Huyton side from 1921, purchased the ground from Lord Derby in the 1920s, became President in 1936 and in a wider sphere was appointed High Sheriff of Lancashire in 1937 and in 1953 President of Lancashire County Cricket Club.[20]

He appears the epitome of the man who had everything; wealth, his family owned collieries just outside Huyton, talent, connections and drive. He was prepared to support the Club financially, guaranteeing any deficit in the tradition of the Eccleses, Alexander and Harry, yet he expected, perhaps reasonably to control things. Not surprisingly people seem to have been happy with this arrangement, whereby they could continue to play cricket in congenial company, at no great personal expense and in pleasant surroundings. And the setting in the 20s and 30s was indeed pleasant. Harry Owen, a life member and Vice-President, who played throughout this period describes the Huyton of the 1930s as

> "a cricket club surrounded by trees. You could stand on the square and not see a building other than the vicarage through the trees and the tower of the church. There was a path from the vicarage to the ground and the Vicar used to come down every Saturday along this path to watch the game over his gate."[21]

There is little doubt either that Huyton continued to be a select club. The occupations of the players in the 1930s team show this clearly:—

W.G.Milne	Corn trade	H.N.Owen	Accountant
W.L. Shaw	Cotton broker	W.Brumpton	Insurance
R.McEntegart	Meat purveyor	B.A.Williams	Funeral Director
J.K.Edmondson	Cotton merchant	E.W.Gittins	Bank Manager
W. Handbidge	Insurance	C.L.Moore	Scientist
B.Barrell	Cricket professional	A.D.Milne	Bank official[22]

Yet the select nature of the Club was not ensured by any rules, nor do there appear to have been occasions when people were refused membership. In the words, again, of Harry Owen,

> "they wouldn't have applied. They would consider that they weren't up to the standard of the Club, both as cricketers and socially but more socially. There was one man, a coal miner, a very good cricketer who kept wicket. He stayed for a couple of years, but he spoke a different language."[23]

There was in the town by this time another cricket club, Huyton Recs, and presumably those who felt themselves "as cricketers and socially" inferior played there.

It is perhaps more than coincidental that a great decline in interest, both locally and nationally, occurred in 1950s and 1960s when clubs like Huyton continued to try to remain select whilst in the country as a whole people no longer accepted the criteria on which these notions were based.

Huyton's strength, in its first 100 years, had lain with its wealthy benefactors yet the resultant ad hoc system of management

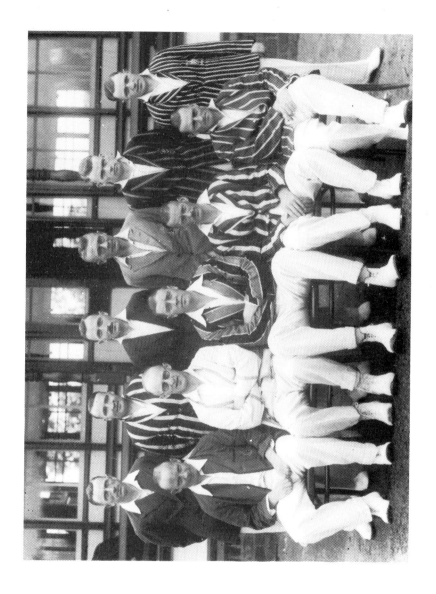

HUYTON CRICKET CLUB 1st XI, 1934
Back:
Barrell, B. Williams, W. Hannridge, C.A. Hunter, G. Gleave, H.W. Owen
Front:
A.D. Milne, C.L. Moore, J.K. Edmundson (Capt.), E.W. Gittens, R. McEntegart

ultimately contributed to its decline. By the 1960s rising wages and inflation made it impossible for a crisis to be solved simply by individuals putting their hands down more deeply into their pockets. Huyton was by no means alone in this dilemma and the same problem can be seen at many other clubs. Harold Wolfe recalls going to an Annual General Meeting at Neston in the early 1950s when it was mentioned that the club needed to purchase a new mowing machine and there was some competition among the members for the privilege of paying for it.[24] Not long afterwards Neston suffered a severe financial crisis, from which they were eventually saved by the opportunity to start from scratch when the rather dilapidated wooden pavilion burnt down. Harold also recalls a discussion with Brian Jones in the early 1960s where the latter observed,

> "our pavilion is falling down at Chester — we are suffering from the sins of our fathers, because in the old days all the wealthy men in Chester, all members of the club, they never thought about the future, never thought about planning and now the pavilion is decrepit — we've got no money and we haven't got the wealthy members either."[25]

At Southport, we have seen already how the control of the Club in the hands of one man however wealthy and benevolent tended to foster an ostrich-like attitude among the membership to the harsh realities of club management.[26]

The cricket-loving benefactors have gone and been replaced by hard-headed accountants from the breweries. Any money they are prepared to invest in improving cricket clubs is expected to return a profit and any benefit to the game is of secondary importance.

At Huyton all these changes were more disastrous than in clubs where the brewery accountants could see potential, for they coincided with changes in the surrounding environment which made the Club a considerably less pleasant one to belong to, and as a result a change in the number and type of people who wished to play there.

REFERENCES

1. *Huyton Cricket and Bowling Club* 1860-1960. Centenary Souvenir Programme (Daily Post Printers 1960), p.5.
2. Minute Book of the Huyton C.C. (1860-63), 7th May 1860, deposited at Huyton Library.
3. This was probably a newspaper soubriquet derived from the earlier club.
4. A.G. Colwell, *Beautiful Huyton with Roby* (1980), p.51.
5. Census 1861, on microfilm at Huyton Library.
6. Scorebook of Huyton C.C. 1860, deposited at Huyton Library
7. Minute Book (1860-63), op. cit., 7th May 1860.

8. Ibid., listed at the back.
9. Ibid, 1st October 1861.
10. *Huyton Cricket and Bowling Club 1860-1960*, op. cit., p.6.
11. Accounts of Huyton Cricket and Bowling Club, June 1866 deposited at Huyton Library.
12. Ibid., October 1870.
13. Minute Book of Huyton C.C. (1915-19), 19th May 1915, deposited at Huyton Library.
14. Ibid., 22nd February 1917.
15. Ibid., 26th February 1918.
16. Ibid., 25th February 1919.
17. 1920 — played 21 won 16 drawn 3 lost 2.
    1921 — played 22 won 14 drawn 4 lost 4.
    1922 — played 22 won 13 drawn 3 lost 6.
    1923 — played 20 won 10 drawn 3 lost 7.
18. J.A. Mangan, *Social Darwinism, Sport and English Upper Class Education* (paper delivered to the Inaugural Conference of The British Society of Sport. March 1982), p.20.
19. Quoted in Mangan, op. cit., pp.26-28, and note 105.
20. *Huyton Cricket and Bowling Club 1860-1960*, op. cit., p.16.
21. Interview with H. Owen, (Huyton C.C.), 18th November 1982.
22. Ibid.
23. Ibid.
24. Interview with H. Wolfe, (retired sports editor of the Liverpool Echo), 10th November 1982.
25. Ibid.
26. See Chapter 3, pp. 51-54.

CHAPTER SIX

The Professionals

In the Liverpool Competition, the era of the professionals ended in 1939. Most clubs were in no position when cricket resumed after the War to afford both a professional and a groundsman. A few did employ groundsman/professionals for a time and there have been occasions when a wealthy member paid for one in the hope of bringing his Club success. On this basis, the Formby president in 1960s paid for young Lancashire groundstaff to play for his club on occasions when they were not required by the county, but it brought no great success and the experiment was not repeated elsewhere. There have, also, been rumours from time to time that such and such a player was receiving 'boot money', either to come to a club or as an incentive not to leave. As the players under suspicion were often only marginally better than average, these rumours caused little disquiet.

The Competition unlike the other northern leagues, where at least one professional is mandatory, has no constitution and thus no regulations, if one accepts the rulings that the tea interval should last 20 minutes and that only grade 'A' balls should be used. A club, therefore, could employ as many professionals as it wished even today, although few clubs, in this century, ever had more than one. Cost, necessity and the amateur ethos have always been the determining factors. Chester Boughton Hall, the only club never to have employed a professional, was a good example of this.

Whatever doubts exist about the early days of other clubs, Chester was at its inception a very select gentleman's club. The owner and occupant of Boughton Hall, Mr. John Thompson was a wealthy businessman educated at Rossall and Trinity College, Cambridge. In 1873 he converted part of his grounds into a cricket field and invited friends to play there under his captaincy. There was no subscription and Thompson met all playing expenses as he continued to do for the next ten years. This pleasant arrangement changed, when Boughton Hall became a successful cricket club and as a consequence the number of matches and the distances travelled increased. The cost became too high for one man and the Club was put on a more orthodox footing with Mr. Thompson as president.[1] But the view of cricket as a game for amateurs prevailed. Not only would Mr. Thompson not countenance the employment of a professional, he would not even allow other teams to bring one to Boughton Hall. In later years when his influence had waned, Chester had such a strong team, often providing a good half of the Cheshire County team and perhaps more importantly such good amateur bowlers, that it had no need of a playing professional. It was felt that to employ one would simply deprive a paying club member of a game. The final factor was that, despite its success in cricketing terms, it was never a wealthy club and in the era between the wars when the professionals in the Competition were probably at their best, it simply could not afford one.[2] That the members were correct in their judgement can be seen in the record during this period. From 1923-39 they played 276 games in the Liverpool Competition and of these they won 156 and only lost 67.[3]

Broadly speaking there are three types of professionals in the leagues if one discounts the 'super stars'. The young men on the way up who move on to county and even international cricket; the older men whose county careers are at an end, and the group which constitutes the majority. These may be better than average club cricketers, who are either not quite good enough to make the step into full time professionalism or who have careers which make it impossible to do so, or men who see their earnings from cricket on a Saturday afternoon as supplementary. Which of these types a club decides to employ depends very much on availability, contacts, how much it is prepared to pay and what services it expects.

Generally however, the Competition clubs in choosing a professional tended to be conservative, preferring the man with a long consistent record whether it was at county level or in another league. Few are the examples of men gaining their spurs on Merseyside to go on to greater things. Southport employed for one year in 1901, A.R. Warren a young man from the Derbyshire groundstaff, a fast bowler who subsequently played for England against Australia and took 5 for 57 in one innings.[4] This seems to have been very much a result of the contacts which Southport had, through two brothers, Frank and Walter Sugg, who played both for the Club and Derbyshire. Warren's successor, Jack Young, also came from this county. A more familiar name is that of Len Hopwood, the professional at Wallasey in 1926 and 1927, who later gained Test rank and who scored, for Lancashire, over 15,000 runs and took 672 wickets. He remains the only Lancastrian who has twice performed the double of a 1,000 runs and 100 wickets in a season. However it is, in some ways, an exaggeration to describe him as on the way up when he came to Wallasey as he had already scored a century in first class cricket. It was a disagreement with Lancashire over terms which had brought him to Competition cricket.[5]

Of those whose county careers were at an end, there are numerous examples of which Eddie Bates is but one. Already approaching 50 years of age when he left Glamorgan, he was still able to score over

1,000 runs including five centuries and 111 wickets for Neston in 1933.[6] To put this and other records into perspective, only two men have scored a 1,000 runs in the Competition since the 1950s and there are only a handful of bowlers who annually take even 50 wickets nowadays. There was Frank Dennis of Oxton, an ex Yorkshire player, Bill Hickmott of Wallasey who had previously played for both Kent and Lancashire, but probably the most famous was Harry Tyldesley of Oxton. Tyldesley had played for many years with Lancashire and had been on an M.C.C. tour to Australia and New Zealand in 1922/3, before he arrived at Oxton in 1924. In the seven seasons he played there he took an astonishing total of 822 wickets. Not so surprisingly, Oxton topped the Competition table for five of these years.[7]

There are several fine examples of the third type of professional. Many certainly could, had they wished, have made the grade in first class cricket and their records are often as good as those of Tyldesley and Hopwood. There was Walter Davies, whom we have already met on the ground staff at Huyton in 1915. After the War he moved to Hightown where he never missed a game in 21 years and is still the only man to have hit a double hundred this century.[8] Jack Threlfall with Southport from 1934-38, who was one example of the cricket mercenary with the number of clubs for whom he played. Jack Bartley, who later became a Test match umpire, was originally at Birkenhead Park and later Ormskirk. He regularly took in excess of 130 wickets a year in Competition games and his prodigious ability is perhaps best illustrated in the 1938 match for Ormskirk against Liverpool. The Liverpool side was possibly at its most powerful since the days of the Steel brothers, with four University Blues, Brocklebank, Ledgard, Barlow and Dyson plus the ex Lancashire captain Jack Barnes and two youngsters Ken Cranston, later Lancashire and England and Alex Husband. Bartley bowled them out for 66 taking 9 for 29, although it must be added that Liverpool still retained their unbeaten 1938 recorded by dismissing Ormskirk for 62.[9]

It may seem specious to single out one man, but Ben Barrell seems to have possessed all the best qualities of this type of professional. His career with Huyton covered all the inter-war years and in this period

"he scored 9343 runs and took 2,020 wickets, did the hat trick four times, scored two centuries and five times exceeded 90. With three exceptions he took 100 wickets against all Competition clubs, including all ten against Hightown in 1921 and many times nine in an innings."[10]

He was made a life member of the Club, became 1st XI umpire and played bowls there until his death at the age of 80. "One of the best men you could meet and one of the district's most outstanding cricketers."[11]

Unlike many of the other top professionals of the 1930s, Ben Barrell was also the groundsman and Club coach. Four nights a week he spent at least two hours at the nets, having worked on the ground all day sometimes starting as early as 6 o'clock in the morning. Harry Owen, a Huyton Vice-President, who played in the 1930s describes some of Barrell's other duties.

"He prepared all the team's kit. The 11 players of the 1st team would have their nets during the week and often their togs were left lying around. Ben packed all their bags and on Saturday morning they'd be loaded. We had various methods of getting them to away games, but it was all under Ben's supervision. It might be loaded into a taxi or a trailer to a car or taken to the station and he would be responsible for those 11 bags and the players would open their bags and there was their tackle. And after the game, he might not actually pack the bags, but he'd be responsible for seeing they got back. He cleaned their kit and he got a small payment for that — I think he might have got about five shillings (from each man) for the season. He cleaned their pads and boots. I remember one long standing 1st team player, McEntegart, saying that as soon as Ben finishes, he was retiring."[12]

In this Barrell was much more like the 19th century professionals who all had jobs which combined in differing degrees the duties of groundsman, net bowler, coach and player. Some of the men were primarily groundsmen who played a bit and bowled to the members. Others were engaged for their skills as cricketers and worked mainly on the square often with assistants to do the outfield. Few indeed were the men who were excellent players, groundsmen and coaches, and each club chose according to its particular needs and the money available. Thus a wealthy club like Liverpool had less need of a star playing professional, for they had talented amateurs in plenty. The professional staff at Aigburth, sometimes as many as five, were there to bowl to the members and assist in looking after the ground. Several of them were good players who were allowed leave, usually unpaid, to play for their counties and did play in Club and Ground games, but only to perform what the amateurs considered the chore of bowling. In contrast the smaller clubs such as Oxton, Southport, Formby and Hightown needed their professional to be a well above average player, if only to even things up when they played the likes of

Liverpool, Sefton and Birkenhead Park.

Not surprisingly there was considerable variation in the wages the professionals received. The following wage list shows merely the highest and lowest weekly wage in each decade and is limited to those clubs which have provided information. It must also be remembered that they were only employed for half a year, at most probably 27 weeks.

1860s £1.5s. (J. Sherman Huyton)
1870s £1.1s (Faulkner Oxton) — £1.13s (J. Unsworth Huyton)
1880s £1.15s (Huffen Ormskirk) — £3. (Liverpool ground bowlers)
1890s £1.5s (Kirwan Wallasey) — £3.3s (Liverpool ground bowlers)
1910s £2.10s plus 10s for 50 runs and 5/- for 5 wickets (E. Hall Neston)
1920s £6. (L. Hopwood Wallasey)
1930s £6.10s (B. Barrell Huyton) — £9. (F. Dennis Oxton)[13]

Of course these bare figures do not tell the whole story. One cannot, for example, equate Hopwood's £6, basically for a Saturday afternoon's work and a bit of coaching with Barrell's similar wage but totally different duties in the same period. Additionally there were often, written into their contracts, other sources of income. Many had a benefit game which, with the large crowds often as many as 5,000 at Sefton or Birkenhead, and donations from the members, could realise annually in excess of £100. There may have been also incentive bonuses similar to Hall's of Neston, although the practice, common in the Lancashire leagues, of passing a collection box round the crowd after a 'performance' does not seem to have occurred. A Competition crowd could thus sit comfortably until the end of the match, there being no necessity to drift towards the gate as the local hero prepared to win the game and reach his 50. Other clubs allowed their professional to organise a franchise through sports outfitters for the sale of equipment. One notorious professional at Southport in the early thirties, who was described by the secretary of the time as "a terrible fellow — an absolute rogue", took advantage of this sytem.

> "All the tradesmen closed their doors to him. James Fay (the local sports outfitters) supplied him with bats to sell, but was left whistling for his money."[14]

This man apart, they do seem generally to have been honest, reliable, hard working and often surprisingly loyal employees, considering the wages they received and the hours they worked. We have already seen what Barrell's duties at Huyton, in the inter-war period, were. That they had not changed much over the years is shown in the Ormskirk minutes for 1881, where Huffen's duties are laid down as "keeping the tent (i.e. pavilion) in order, cutting the grass, rolling and repairing the ground and keeping it in good and playable condition. Also that he be at liberty to bowl to the Members of the Club at Half-past four o'clock and during the remainder of the evening."[15]

He also cleaned, packed and looked after the members' kit and played himself on match days.

Admittedly their wages were higher than they would probably have earned outside cricket and in some ways the quality of their life was better than it might have been in industry or agriculture, but they were after all talented people. Their wages scarcely recognised this talent and they were seen very much as club servants, however great their cricketing abilities. At Southport in the 1920s

"they had to address the members as mister and they were there to bowl at the nets when required; in fact, during the afternoon if some boys were home from school (presumably public schoolboys on holiday) and wanted to practice, it was the thing to get the professional to turn out and bowl to them and coach them. The fathers used to give them (the professionals) something in their pockets."[16]

Although an often vital part of the 1st XI, they were at the same time apart. At most of the clubs they had separate changing accommodation and usually entered the field through a different gate. At Liverpool they were not allowed to come up the front steps and were never under any circumstances allowed into the pavilion. In this, some might argue, they were in good company. Up to the 1960s there was a notice at Aigburth, which stated unequivocally "Dogs and Ladies are not allowed in the Pavilion."[17]

Peter Burrell at Oxton makes the point, however, that some of the professionals were

"rather, rough old chaps who didn't want to become part of the social life. They just played their cricket and went away afterwards. I don't think that was because they weren't wanted, I think it was because that's the way they chose to be."

He also recalls an occasion at Liverpool when Harry Tyldesley was the professional and the Oxton captain put his foot down about the business of separate entrances to the field and insisted,

"either my whole side comes down the pavilion steps or my whole side comes in through the professional's entrance. I don't mind which it is, but I'm not having any division between professionals and amateurs in my side."

Sadly however, such were the unbending attitudes of Liverpool that all the Oxton team entered through the professionals gate.[18] This picture of the nowadays staunchly middle class Oxton Club as a hotbed of radicalism is a pleasantly surprising one.

Apart from the extremes of such places as Liverpool, the attitude to the professionals was often a strangely ambivalent one and depended as much on the personality of the professional as on the members themselves. Perhaps this is best illustrated in the description of that most successful of Competition professionals, Ben Barrell.

"At Huyton the professional came out of a separate gate and changed separately. It's not as bad as it might sound especially to a non-cricket lover because a lot of the professionals preferred it that way — to change away from people on their own. I don't think they were worried about coming out of a separate gate. I remember an occasion at Huyton, when Ben had just got a big score — I think 99 actually and he was making his way back. When he got to the pavilion to go into his own entrance, Horace Bryant, the captain, went onto the pavilion steps and beckoned him through the front entrance. That was quite a departure from what usually happened — a kind of privilege accorded to him for his good knock. To put the record straight, Ben Barrell was so well liked and he was a man you'd be proud of anywhere, of taking him to any club. He was a man of great tact, he'd never let you down. He knew when to keep his mouth shut — a quiet sort of individual."[19]

Half a century has passed since the heyday of the professionals and, although other leagues continue to employ them, the Competition is very unlikely to see their type again.[20] Yet the debate still continues especially among those who played and watched cricket before the last war, as to the influence they had on standards. Some like Harold Wolfe would argue that,

"for those who played in or watched games in the Liverpool and District Competition in the thirties, this was the halcyon age — when thousands flocked to Birkenhead Park, Sefton or Bootle to cheer their favourites and barrack the visitors, and the cricket was positive, entertaining and often breathtakingly thrilling. It was the era of the professionals — not world renowned stars such as are found in the Lancashire leagues today, but men who knew their craft and for a modest six or seven pounds a week gave full value in every way. Their presence raised the standard all round and if the professional took 100 wickets during the season, it was not uncommon for the amateurs at the other end to claim his 50 or 60 wickets as well."[21]

Lest it be thought that this was the view of the onlooker rather than the player, Peter Burrell who played in this "halcyon era" feels that

"the professionals quite definitely lifted the standard, partly because you didn't need to have four or five bowlers — people like Tyldesley were never taken off. The wickets were so much better in the Competition that you didn't get the situations which you see in the Lancashire League, where it becomes often no contest at all for the young amateurs facing fast men on variable wickets."[22]

Others would argue that the professionals rather than raising standards and fostering talent among the other players often had the adverse effect. Jack Bennett at Liverpool feels that all that was lost with their disappearance was their coaching ability and their accuracy at net practice.

"But not to play. I had some very salutary lessons facing these pros and I don't think it did me any good at all. The first time I ever walked down these steps to face a pro, it was Jack Bartley. I lasted about four balls, two of them hit me on the inside of the thigh. I was just chicken fodder to him. They were simply too good."[23]

This is the view of a man who played on the best batting wicket on Merseyside.

It is possibly true that the game in the 1930s was more "positive and entertaining" but it is naive to imagine that the simple reintroduction of professionals would bring back those days. So much else has changed. The development of defensive attitudes and the much greater emphasis placed on fielding have both made Saturday afternoon scores much in excess of 200 a rarity. But probably, above all, the importance attached to winning the league, despite its still being a newspaper one has made the game tighter and the desire to entertain has largely disappeared along with the crowds who once demanded it.

Whether the professionals raised standards or hindered progress is a question which will never be satisfactorily answered. The alchemy of memory, as always, leads people to recall only their more glorious deeds. In all probability it hinged on both the type of professional the club employed and the type of person he was. It is difficult to see how the mercenaries, appearing only on a Saturday afternoon, disappearing immediately after the game and changing clubs at the drop of a contract could have offered their fellow players much more than the opportunity to emulate them. Yet the real working professional, in constant attendance and willing to coach and advise the younger men both in the nets and on the field must surely have been of tremendous benefit.

REFERENCES

1. *A Century at Boughton Hall – Chester Boughton Hall Cricket Club 1873-1973* (1973), pp. 1-3.
2. Interview with F. Hack, (President of the Club in 1973), 20th October 1982.
3. *A Century at Boughton Hall,* p.35.
4. K.H. Porter, Twelve Decades of Cricket 1859-1979, Fifth Decade p.10, unpublished copy in the possession of Southport and Birkdale C.C.
5. H. Wolfe, *Wallasey Cricket Club 1864-1964* (1964), p.17.
6. J.H. Gilling, *50 Years of Neston Cricket* (1947), p.16.
7. *Oxton Cricket Club 1875-1975* Centenary handbook (1975), p.7.
8. H. Wolfe — The Fantastic Thirties. Written for the Liverpool Echo but never published (1969), p.2.
9. Ibid., pp. 5-6.
10. Huyton Cricket and Bowling Club 1860-1960 (Daily Post Printers 1960), p.18.
11. Interview with H. Owen (Huyton C.C.), 18th November 1982.
12. Ibid.
13. Information on wages compiled from minute books, accounts and various short histories of Huyton, Ormskirk, Oxton, Wallasey, Southport, Neston, Liverpool, Sefton and Bootle cricket clubs.
14. Interview with K.H. Porter (Secretary of Southport and Birkdale C.C.), November 24th 1982.
15. Minutes of Ormskirk C.C., in the possession of the Club, 6th May 1881.
16. Interview with K.H. Porter, op. cit.
17. Interview with J. Bennett (President of Liverpool C.C.), 30th November 1982.
17. Interview with P. Burrell (President of Oxton C.C.), 20th October 1982.
19. Interview with H. Owen, op. cit.
20. Since writing this in 1982-3 a type of professional has returned to the Competition. Over the past four seasons 1984-7, promising young West Indian cricketers have been sponsored to play for Competition clubs on the Wirral. In 1985 the most successful of these, Winston Benjamin took 106 wickets and over 500 runs for Chester who, not surprisingly, emerged champions. The majority of players, however, doubt both the need for such players and the wisdom of using very fast bowlers on sometimes less than perfect wickets.
21. H.Wolfe, op. cit., p.1.
22. Interview with P. Burrell, op. cit.
23. Interview with J. Bennett, op. cit.

CHAPTER SEVEN

Conclusion

There are today over a hundred cricket clubs of differing sizes throughout Merseyside as there have been for well over a century. From the 19th century records of the three early Southport clubs, Southport, Southport Alexandria and Birkdale which eventually merged to become Southport and Birkdale C.C., 137 different opponents can be identified in the years 1859-95. This is a minimum figure, for there are years for which no records survive. Most of these 137 clubs have long since disappeared and there will also have been others since that time which have come and gone. Several of these early opponents have survived and remained small, vastly important to the few who belong to them, but having little influence beyond this.

Yet many of the 16 Competition Clubs had equally humble beginnings and have prospered if not without their difficult periods. In their early days, especially, their situations were often precarious and their movements from one site to another bear ample testament to this. Whilst they are now, undeniably, the prestige cricket clubs on Merseyside, there are still, as in earlier times, wide differences among them. One has only to compare the opulence of Liverpool with the relative decay of once great clubs like Bootle to see how difficult it is to generalise about them. However, there were certain common qualities which they possessed at different times and to different degrees, and certain common influences which shaped their development. I have tried to bring out these points within the general narrative and they are, here, only briefly restated.

One such influence was undoubtedly the railway network. As it spread it enabled clubs to extend and, thereby, improve their fixtures, but, more importantly, by its creation of suburbs and dormitory towns, it brought with it the middle classes with their predisposition to invest in expensive and time consuming activities such as cricket. The map on page 84 shows the dates when the various railway lines were opened and the years when the Competition Clubs were formed.

All the clubs enjoyed some kind of patronage. This did not come from landed interests whether local gentry or aristocracy. Although the names of the great landowners such as Derby or Sefton have cropped up in this history, it was only as landlords or as figureheads. Lord Skelmersdale apart, there is no evidence of their having been actively involved. The patronage came instead from the middle

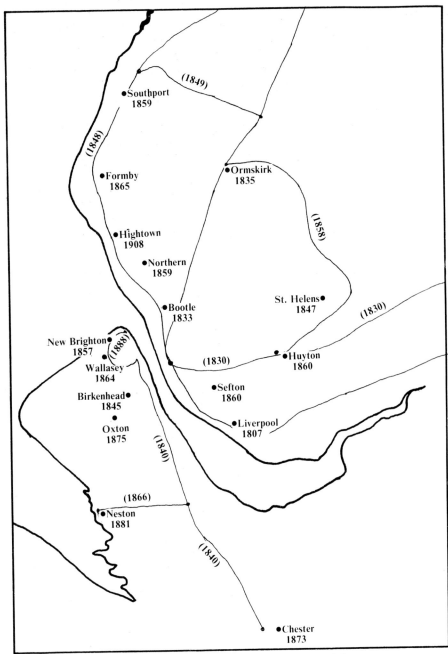

Southport
1859

(1849)

(1848)

Formby
1865

Ormskirk
1835

(1858)

Hightown
1908

Northern
1859

St. Helens
1847

(1830)

Bootle
1833

New Brighton
1857

(1888)

Huyton
1860

(1830)

Wallasey
1864

Sefton
1860

Birkenhead
1845

Oxton
1875

Liverpool
1807

(1840)

(1866)

Neston
1881

(1840)

Chester
1873

The Railway Network and the Competition Clubs.

classes, from the wealthy businessmen, who saw the social advantages of involvement in cricket, just as today membership of the best golf clubs is considered an essential social cachet. But, whatever their motives, they did provide the necessary financial security.

Another common quality was the possession of a suitable ground, large enough, well kept and suitably situated to attract the 'right' type of member and, equally, a good standard of opponent. Locating such a ground may have taken time, but, until this was done, the progress of the club was always impeded. We have also seen the different ways in which clubs, having found a ground, established some security of tenure, whether by long lease, by some special arrangement with the Local Authority or, as in the case of many, by outright purchase.

The desirability of wealthy benefactors has already been mentioned, but for the long term prosperity of the club, money alone was not sufficient. There was also a need for far-sighted administrators, for men who planned ahead. Such men became even more important after the Second World War. Up to 1939, given a good ground, a reasonably comfortable pavilion and people willing to make up the small annual deficits, most could survive as cricket clubs functioning from April to September. Relatively low rates rents and wages ensured that any deficit would be within the compass of their benefactors to correct. Since then, to have any reasonable security, many of the clubs have had to become multi-sports centres, dependent on the income from bar, gambling machines and other money raising activities. Those clubs which have either been unable or unwilling to adapt, like Huyton or Bootle, although they still survive, are leading a strictly hand to mouth existence.

BIBLIOGRAPHY

General

Barker, T.C., *Pilkington Brothers and the Glass Industry* (George Allen and Unwin Ltd., 1960).

Hughes, T., *Tom Brown's School Days* (1857)

Lowerson, J.R., *English Middle Class Sport 1880-1914* (Paper delivered to the Inaugural Conference of the British Society of Sport History, March 1982).

Mangan, J.A., *Social Darwinism, Sport and English Upper Class Education* (Paper delivered to the Inaugural Conference of the British Society of Sport History, March 1982).

Wrigley E.A. and Schofield R.S., *The Population History of England 1541-1871* (Arnold, 1981).

General Cricket

Birley, D., *The Willow Wand* (MacDonald and James, 1979).

Bowen, R., Cricket: *A History of its Growth and Development throughout the world* (Eyre and Spottiswood, 1970).

Brookes, C., *English Cricket* (Weidenfeld and Nicholson, 1978).

Brooking, G.A., (ed), *The Complete History of Liverpool and District versus Colonial and Foreign Teams, First Class Counties and Cambridge University* (T.W. Gornall & Co., 1931).

Kay, J., *Cricket in the Leagues* (Eyre and Spottiswood, 1970).

Kay, J., *A History of County Cricket. Lancashire* (Arthur Barker Ltd., 1972).

Swanton E.W., *Follow On* (Collins, 1977).

Wolfe, H., The Fantastic Thirties (Written for the Liverpool Echo in 1969, but never published).

Local Histories

Bailey, F.A., *A History of Southport* (Angus Downie, 1955).

Barker, T.C. and Harris, J.R., *A Merseyside Town in the Industrial Revolution: St. Helens 1750-1900* (Cass, 1954).

Brooks, R., *Never a Dull Moment: The Bootle Story* (Bootle Corporation, 1968).

Colwell, A.G. *Beautiful Huyton with Roby* (1980).

Woods, E.C. and Brown, P.C., *The Rise and Progress of Wallasey* (Wallasey Corporation, 1960).

Cricket Club Histories

Bootle — Brown, H.S., The History of Bootle Cricket Club (unpublished, 1942).

Chester — Robinson, A., *A Century at Boughton Hall* (1973).

Huyton — *Huyton Cricket and Bowling Club 1860-1960* (1960).

Liverpool — A Sketch of Liverpool Cricket Club (1930).

Neston — Gilling, J.H., *50 Years of Neston Cricket* (1947).

Ormskirk — Stretch, W., *Ormskirk Cricket Club: a few particulars of its Progress and Records (1935).*

Oxton — *Oxton Cricket Club 1875-1975* (1975).

Sefton — *Sefton Cricket Club 1860-1960* (1960).

Southport — Porter, K.H., Twelve Decades of Cricket 1859-79; Being the Story of Southport and Birkdale Cricket Club (1980 Unpublished).

Wallasey — Wolfe, H., *Wallasey Cricket Club 1864-1964* (1964)